Engraved by A.B. Walter, Phila.

yours respectfully
O. S. Pratt

THE

Horse Educator

INTRODUCING

A NEW AND PRACTICAL SYSTEM

OF

EDUCATING HORSES

AND

Breaking up Vicious Habits,

BY

O. S. PRATT.

Containing many valuable recipes as well as an explanation to my class and scholars of the theory they learn of me, for future reference.

ALSO,

REMARKS ON SHOEING

AND THE

RULES OF THE UNION COURSE, L. I.

SEVENTH EDITION.

PHILADELPHIA:
SHERMAN & CO., PRINTERS.

HOW PROF. PRATT WAS WHIPPED

BY THE

BALTIMOREANS.

The amphitheatre of Prof. Pratt, the Horse Educator, at the corner of Green and Pratt Streets, was crowded on Thursday night by an appreciative audience, to witness the education of a number of horses. Near the close of the free exhibition, an interruption occurred by Mr. Murdoch introducing F. P. Stevens, Esq., a member of the Baltimore Bar, who made the following eloquent and pithy speech, in presenting an elaborate whip to Prof. Pratt:

"On behalf of the members of your class in this city, numbering over three thousand, I have been requested to present to you on parting with us, some memento of our high regard for you personally, and of our estimation of your most admirable system of Horse Education. That the instruction you have imparted to us has been valuable and useful, no one of us who own horses would hesitate to testify, not only in your directions as to the management, education, and treatment of the horse, but in developing to us in the numerous lectures, the disposition and nature of the noble animal. That your course of instruction has been popular among us, the numerical strength of the class convinces you, and I take great pleasure in presenting you this token of friendship and good will, and hope that you may ever recur with pleasure to your visit to the Monumental City, and as soon as your engagements will permit, we may have the pleasure of seeing you again."

The Professor not having yet become "educated" to whippings of the like kind, was taken by surprise, briefly returned his sincere thanks for the token, and made other remarks suitable to the occasion. The whip was made at the large establishment of Messrs. Millikin & Sons, and is one of the finest ever produced by them, the handle being of elaborately carved ivory, finely chased gold mounting, with one of the handsomest of black whalebone stocks, knotted, and the knots pointed by alternate clusters of ivory and pearl sets, presenting a beautiful appearance. The Professor's monogram is on the handle, on which also will be engraved the names of some of the members, and the number of the class.

The following are the names of the Committee:

Gen. J. S. Berry,	Enoch Pratt,
Alee Brown,	Geo. W. Robinson,
R. Stockart Mathews,	Henry Tyson,
Ichabod Jean,	F. L. Lawrence,
Marshall Gouldsborrough,	F. P. Stevens,

Part of Baltimore Class, numbering 3504,
February, 1871.

PRATT,

THE GREAT HORSE TRAINER.

You man of sixty, with no vital force,
How you would like to drive your noble horse;
How you'd delight to take the country air,
And free yourself and wife of ev'ry care;
But you are feeble, and your colt is shy,—
He starts at ev'ry object that is nigh?
Then go to PRATT, to his horse-training school,
And he will gladly teach you how to rule.

Young ladies, who are blessed with ample wealth
And sigh for saddles to improve the health—
How you would like to ride at morn and eve;
But you have fear your horse will take his leave,
He'll kick, or run, or jump, or rear, or start,
And you, for saddle pleasures, fail at heart.
Then let your brothers go to PRATT, and find
How vicious horses are made tame and kind.

You jockey, daily driving on the course,
And making all your income from the horse,—
You find that there is much you'd like to know;
There's something wrong—your balky horse don't go,
Your knowledge fails to serve you, and you see
That men are doubting your ability:
Then go to PRATT, and he will quickly show
Those points that make the jockey's bosom glow.

You countryman, with "nag" that rules the barn,
Inflicting on you ev'ry kind of harm;
With nag that drives your hired man away,
And fills the plow-boy with a deep dismay,—
Obtain the knowledge you would never sell—
Facts worth far more than human tongue can tell.
PRATT is the man to teach you, he'll unfold
The science worth a purse well fill'd with gold.

You blacksmith, wondering what you will do,—
You man in terror of the horse you shoe;
You man with wife, who has a fev'rish head,
Through fear a kick will send you to the dead:
Why don't you give your family relief,
And free them from this daily chance of grief?
Go learn of PRATT, your woe will have an end,
He'll teach the facts, on which you may depend.

This PRATT will take your full-blood, fierce and wild,
And forty minutes find him like a child;
Your blooded charger, full of trick and balk,
Is taught to do most ev'rything but talk.
He'll nod for "yes," and shake his head for "no,"
Lie down, go lame, back, stop, or forward go;
He'll pick up kerchiefs, kiss you, and he'll seem
Some human friend with intellect supreme.

This PRATT will give your lazy horse a fire,
Your rampant steed he'll teach you how to tire;
He'll stop his cribbing, he will stop all tricks
That put both horse and owner "in a fix."
He'll make you *master*, fill your soul with joy,
To see a horse soon governed by a boy;
And this great art you readily secure,
On terms to suit the purses of the poor.

And who is PRATT? He's an electric man;
With him the motto is—I *will* and *can!*
And New York Ledger Bonner, and a host,
Proclaim he is a man of whom to boast.
I, as a pupil, have more "horse" in store,
Than learned from ev'ry other source before.
Then go to PRATT—go to his ring and *see*,
And you will swear to all you've read from me.

THE CANING

OF

Professor O. S. Pratt.

MONDAY eve, the 21st of February, 1870, will long be remembered by those citizens who are interested in horse education. During the free exhibition of Professor O. S. Pratt, at his Horse-Educating Tent-School, on Eighth street, below Vine, our townsman poet, Elmer Ruan Coates, very unexpectedly entered the ring, and, holding up a magnificently elaborated golden-headed cane, surprised the Professor in an eloquent address, which we can give only in synopsis.

Mr. Coates declared that all nations, in all ages, have delighted to honor the meritorious. The analytic mind of Greece was promoted to the Academy and Groves of the same, while bright intellects gave homage and quaffed gems of lore.

The school-boy quoted Roman, if a victor passed under the triumphal arch, bowing to popular plaudits. If a poet, he was laureated; if philosophic, oratoric, or mechanical, he had his meed of honor from proper sources. Even the Tartars were grateful, and Tamerlane, the great Usbeck, was elevated in proportion to merit.

The American Indian who exhibits military strategy, is chosen chief *pro merito,* and leads the painted warriors. The highly-cultured United States never forgets the truly great. Here the statesman, poet, orator, lawyer, divine, artist, man of science or mechanism, is both courted and remunerated. Our worthy dead live in hearts, monuments, statues, statuettes, and oil. The living, acting man of the day is recipient of both newspaper glory and *material* recognition.

Taking the Professor by the hand, he continued: My friend, a full consideration of gratitude has timely and most heartily determined your large class to offer this El-Dorado-headed cane. Sir, we recognize you as the greatest equestrian educator in the world. Your humble servant is proud of his recent acquisition. You have enabled the palsied old man to ride in safety; you allow the old lady to drive minus the fear of a broken neck; the young lady or horse-loving master can now indulge saddle pleasures, knowing the animal thoroughly subdued by some member of your class.

Every vicious trait a horse can possess is thoroughly cured by your unequaled skill. You are a practicalist, a utilitarian, an educator in one of the most necessary and recreative branches of polite culture. Indeed, a logical lawyer could raise a fine issue relative to the comparative merits of your skill and that of the statesman. Disparaging no sphere, I would say that the live, practical, successful man in any avocation, is the person we need and the individual we will honor.

Your grateful class, at this date numbering 2523, are of my sentiments, and now delegate me to tender this beautiful present—not as a *quid pro quo*, but merely as a memento. My dear sir, I trust it will be very long ere you require this as a physical staff. But, when that period does come, may it equally subserve the mental and heart-man, and aid in happy retrospect of Philadelphia, Philadelphians, and your admiring class—a class that mainly hails you as both a high-toned, social gentleman and the horse educator of the age. [Great applause.]

The Professor, receiving the cane, bowing, and somewhat tremulous with emotion, responded as follows:

"What! gentlemen, can it be that, after your many kind attentions, I am to receive a further testimonial of your regard, and another reminder of pleasant times passed with you?—times that certainly I never can forget.

"Words cannot express my feelings on this occasion. Therefore, I sincerely return you thanks."

Here terminated a most pleasant affair, with thunders of demonstration.

The cane bears the following: "A tribute to merit. To Professor O. S. Pratt, from his Philadelphia class, numbering 2523."

TESTIMONIALS TO PROF. O. S. PRATT,

THE

HORSE EDUCATOR OF THE WORLD.

To PROFESSOR O. S. PRATT:

We, the undersigned, members of your Washington class, appreciate the value of the very necessary knowledge which you have imparted to us, during your sojourn at the National Metropolis, and we are convinced that your method of educating the horse and reforming his vicious habits *by kind and gentle treatment*, is the only TRUE SYSTEM.

As a mark of our estimation of the service rendered us, we beg your acceptance of the accompanying testimonial, and our sincere wishes for your continued success, health, and happiness.

H. D. Cooke,
A. B. Mullett,
Robt. Allen, Brev. Maj. Gen. U.S.A.,
M. G. Emery,
L. E. Middleton,
J. R. P. Gleeson, M.D.,
L H. Schneider,
Clark Mills,
M. H. Prince,
E. M. King,
O. E. Babcock, U.S.A.,
Count Catacazy,
Rev. Dr. J. P. Newman,
Lewis J. Davis,
W. T. Sherman, U.S.A.,
Thomas B. Florence,
H. Dwight Smith,
B. H. Stinemetz,
F. H. Gasswells,
S. Wakeman,
H. R. Rathbone,
M. Michler, U.S.A.,
Col. V. E. Van Koerben,
Geo. W. Allen,
Wm. O. Avery,
John Sherwood,
Wm. Latchford,
Mills Dean,
J. C. Howard,
H. W. Read.

Committee:

COL. W. OWEN. W. S. SHEPHERD. R. M. CHARLTON

The Philadelphia, Baltimore, and Washington Classes

Presented him with a magnificent Diploma, Gold Medal, Cane, and Whip, as a testimonial to his genius. The Cane is a splendid carved and gold-headed one. The Whip has a richly carved ivory handle, heavy mounted with gold, and inlaid with pearl.

THE CANE HAS THE FOLLOWING INSCRIPTION :

A Tribute of Merit

To O. S. Pratt, from his Philadelphia Class, 4886,

February 22d, 1870.

Gen. Geo. Cadwalader,	Mayor Fox,
Joseph W. Drexel,	Morgan & Orr,
Robert Hamill,	Alex. McAdams, M.D.,
William Piper, M.D.,	E. Ruan Coates,
Robert Grey,	Jacob Peters,
George W. Simmons,	William Chapman, Jr.,
Alexander Siddell,	Samuel Cressman.

Committeee.

THE ENGRAVING ON THE WHIP IS AS FOLLOWS:

February 10, 1871.

Testimonial to Professor O. S. Pratt.

Gen. J. S. Berry,	Enoch Pratt,
A. Browen,	George W. Robinson,
R. Stockart Matthews,	Henry Tyson,
Icabod Jean,	F. L. Lawrence,
F. P. Stevens,	Marshall Goldsborough.

Part of Committee.

Class of 3505 in 65 days.

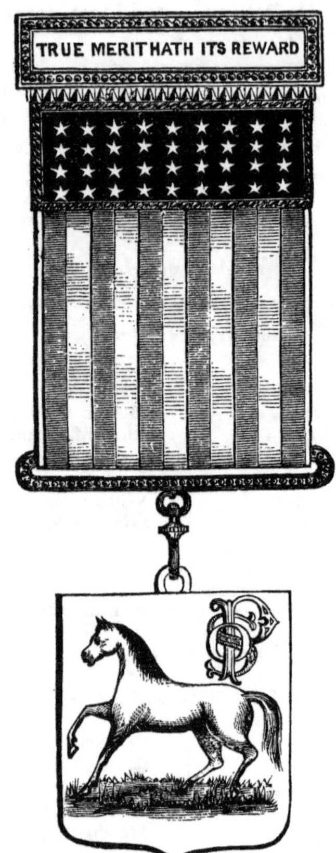

GOLD MEDAL PRESENTED BY WASHINGTON CLASS,

2503 IN 63 DAYS.

PREFACE.

IT is not too much to say, that not one horse in a hundred, if one in a thousand, in the United States is ever properly broken; or one in fifty, when offered for sale as a finished horse, entered in the merest rudiments of his education. Horses are rarely actively, and almost never savagely vicious Nothing more than this, as a general thing, is required. If a horse will carry his rider without kicking him over his head, or draw him in his wagon or carriage, without kicking it to chivers; if he will go off at a walk, increase his speed to the top of his gait, and stop again, when pulled upon, without running away; if he will hold back going down hill, and more particularly, if he will stand at a door without tying, he is held to be fully broken, and is willingly received, credited and paid for as such. It is needless to say that such a horse is far from being broken at all, especially from being well broken, as a perusal of the contents of this book will convince the most skeptical.

AUTO-BIOGRAPHICAL.

I WAS born in the county of Genesee, State of New York, the "Garden of the World." I amused myself in my younger days by taming and educating animals of the small kind or order. At the age of twelve years I had a caravan, on a small scale, of trained and tamed coons, crows, squirrels, dogs, rabbits, &c. Such an innate desire had I to see to what perfection the education of animals could be brought, that it became my constant study. And as I advanced in years, the noble horse claimed my attention, and the subject of subduing him by kindness, and in a practical manner, has for some time occupied my thoughts. The result of my observations and study are given in the pages of this volume.

THE

HORSE EDUCATOR.

INTRODUCTORY REMARKS.

THIS book contains the best known method of educating, training and taming horses; it is a system conceded by all before whom it has been practised, as perfect in all its points. Some very valuable ideas differ from R. P. Hamilton, the most important of which is bitting a colt, and has never before been published. I shall also give a few remarks on shoeing, and some valuable recipes for the cure of various diseases horses are subject to.

My object in placing this work before the public is to obliterate many erroneous ideas embraced at the present day by persons who are now ignorant of the fact (and will be till they receive instructions as taught by me), that a theory is necessary to success in the management of a horse. No matter how simple the means used, so long as it brings about the desired effect. Experience teaches us to simplify the process of handling horses, both for their good and the benefit to be derived therefrom.

In this volume I purpose to give explicit directions in regard to the practice of this system, and the means used by me in educating and subduing every horse, thereby showing the secret of my success; showing the system is not only superior to all others in the effects it produces, but that, if practised, it is a never-failing remedy for all vicious and unmanageable horses; also, as being the only safe, sure and *reliable* way of educating colts, and if always used and practised, we shall have no more runaways, no more kicking or balky horses. I firmly believe that all the vicious habits horses have are taught them through the ignorance of their owners or trainers, and it is only through patient study and perseverance that common sense teaches us a better practice than was ever before given to the public. To show the horeseman's superiority over him is the first point to be gained; teaching him that you are "man, and he the horse," that through your better judgment you have over him perfect control; that his business is simply to do your bidding; an object which can in no way be attained except as you first gain submission on his part, through patience and kindness, with a thorough knowledge of a theory both easy and simple to practice, incurring slight expense. Such an one you receive at my hands. So easy is it in its use that a boy ten years of age can, with its assistance, manage the most ugly and vicious of horses with ease and safety, throwing them from ten to twenty times a minute, with his hands in his pockets.

Persons joining my class have the advantage of *buying* the knowledge which has been acquired by years of study as well as the experience of my own experimenting, as it is a well-known fact that physicians hear of different remedies having been used with success for a disease seemingly beyond their control. They conclude to try them as an experiment on their patient, with successful results, and are thereby heralded as the wonder of the age and benefactors of mankind. Thus it is with us. We have tried, and have found a remedy for the vexations incident to the management of the noble, but much abused horse. We call ourselves the horse's friend, because in the use of our instructions he is kindly taught what is required of him. He is first taught that he must succumb to the will of his master. He is then caressed. By showing him that only kindness towards him is intended, he is made to understand what is desired of him, and he is at once your obedient slave.

There are now many works before the public on this all-important subject, and many different systems taught and practised which have failed to please the people. And why? First, because they have failed to make their theory simple to practice, and easy to comprehend, many times using cruel means, thereby disabling the animal, and rendering him unfit for use. The carrying into practice of many of these systems is expensive, the articles for use difficult to procure, and, in the use of them, much muscular strength is required. Therefore, they are seldom tried more than once. I have the advantage over those who have preceded me, of having witnessed their failure, have sought to learn the cause, and guard against the same disaster, till I am now able to introduce an improvement over them all. It is not necessary for me to say this; it is testified to by all the best horsemen in the country. My reputation is so thoroughly established that it is only necessary to let it be known when and where I will give instructions to a class, and, on my arrival, from one to four hundred stand ready to purchase tickets. It matters not how many systems they already know, or how many intimate friends they may have in this business, for whom they desire success. They are each and every one ready to testify to the superiority of this system over all they have ever witnessed, and add that it is labor-saving, and nothing but fun to practice, and before the instructions are half over are satisfied that they have received more than the worth of their money, and would not again be placed in ignorance of it for twenty times the price paid. Not a day passes but I am told that I am doing more good than any one man in this country, by teaching men how to save their own and other's lives, by educating their horses not to kick when any obstacle touches their heels, and to stop, as though shot, at the word of command. You are aware that no medicine is used by me. Notwithstanding skeptics look on in wonder at the result of my practice on horses brought to me to handle, known to be untrue; see me drive them in the street without quarter-straps, ten rods ahead of me; stop and start them, at the word of command, and back the vehicle with their heels, having seemingly forgotten how to kick, or that they ever had the habit. This, outsiders say, must be the effect of medicine, and will not last. But you, as members of my class, know better, and furthermore, that I practice nothing which is not explained to the class, and that every member can perform the same feats, not only on their own, but on every horse that can be produced, no matter what habits of an evil nature they may be addicted to.

It is desirable that colts should all be educated in the manner I teach, that they may never be ugly or have any bad habits to break up. The secret of having so many bad horses in this country is bad management or neglect when they are young. Horses are taught to be ugly, because they are caressed at the wrong time, and whipped for doing just what they have been taught by their master, who has unconsciously ruined them. And after these habits are once contracted, it is very hard to have a remedy to apply,—a physician to apply to. My system is the needed remedy.

Persons having travelled over the road with an inferior system are no stumbling-block for me, because my reputation travels faster than I do, and my friends are made by hearing of me before I arrive in town, and I am welcomed as their benefactor. I am constantly in receipt of letters from various places, soliciting me to come and give them instruction. I travel slowly, and hope to give the citizens of every town in each county an opportunity to learn this system, for it is a fact that more attention is going to be paid to horses and their management than ever before, because the study has at last reached perfection.

In my free exhibitions I show that a horse may be taught to do almost anything but talk. My favorite horse, known as Tom Thumb, or the Ladies' Pet, will answer any direct question as readily as a child, and with equal understanding of what I expect him to do. He is said to be the best trained or educated horse ever shown in this part of the country, and the only one ever seen to walk on his knees, which he does with ease; although it is a feat difficult to perform. He is so perfectly under my control that not a motion of mine during the entertainment escapes his notice; thus, he is prompt in his tricks. Naturally possessing a superior intellect and keen perception, he has been, perhaps, more easily educated than many could have been; but so far as the principles are concerned, any person can teach his own horses to do the same thing, by adhering strictly to the explicit directions herein contained. I have also a white stallion, known as the North Star, educated to drive without reins, guided wholly by the motion of the whip, I do not often exhibit him, because this is not what people care to see. It has been practised through the country by persons teaching a very different system. It is not desirable to me that this system be classed in that capacity, as it must be if I give the same exhibition, nor is it in any way desirable to break horses to drive in this manner, which it is both simple and easy to do, but I deem it more commendable and practicable to teach a horse to drive safely *with reins* under good subjection, spirit unimpaired. The beauty of a horse, aside from his formation of body, is his spirit and ambition, at the same time submission to his master, his word being law, and although it is almost impossible to convince thorough horsemen that they do not know all concerning the horse and his management, when once they can be prevailed upon to witness an explanation of my theory, they are my best advertisers; being known in their community to possess superior knowledge of all the improved systems which have previously been practised, they are so pleased to find something different, and so perfect in all its points, that they at once urge others to come and be benefited also, and it is thought that if we can teach such men anything we must indeed know something worth learning. Were it not that it would occupy too much space, I would give for your perusal some of the many testimonials which have been presented to me during my travels.

But as I do not expect any to peruse this book who have not previously obtained thorough instruction of this system, it is not necessary for me to say what I can do; but merely to explain the manner, through which the good results are produced, for your future reference.

REMARKS FOR YOUR STUDY.

WHEN you have taught your horses what is required of them, and appealed to their understanding by convincing them that with submission on their part, kindness is received, the one great point is gained. A horse or a dog may be taught almost anything, provided you always use precisely the same idea. Show him what you mean, and have the patience to repeat it often enough, always bearing in mind that for us to comprehend another's meaning by motions is very difficult, and we do not expect them to have the reasoning powers which we possess; still, I do believe them to be reasoning creatures, possessing a keen perception of right and wrong. Were it not so, they would not so readily learn to refrain from doing that for which they have been punished, or to do the bidding of those they love, and by whom they have been caressed. They possess strong affections, and, in a degree, manifest them in accordance with the amount of affection demonstrated by their master. It is also true, they know, by instinct, a good man from a cruel one. Also, that they are quite as well aware, when being driven by a coward, as is the driver himself or herself, as the case may be.

I have often heard it remarked that a horse might be ever so gentle, yet would invariably act nervously when being driven by a lady. Have been asked why it was? It is simply this: the horse knows his advantage and realizes her natural timidity, and when he really ought to act the best is almost unmanageable. But, if a horse is in the habit of being petted and fondled by a lady, he soon learns to love and follow her, demonstrating the principle that for himself love is the reward.

The effects of rude treatment are noticeable particularly on horses of a sensitive, ambitious nature; such either fret, or are dangerous when subjected to the management of an impulsive, irritable groom, though extremely docile and safe to a careful, patient person. The great extremes of disposition and character in horses show a peculiar adaptation for different purposes and requirements. The slow, dull, coarse-grained horse, naturally adapted for the cart or plow, cannot bear the active exertion necessary to great speed, while those of a higher spirit would not submit patiently to this slow drudgery. No animal has a keener intuition of the feelings, or is more easily encouraged to viciousness by the indications of fear, or more forcibly held in check by a fearless, confident expression of manner than the horse. It is not, however, to be inferred that not "being afraid of a horse" is by any means to be considered fool-hardiness; courage and confidence should be dictated by the danger shown. The expression of the eye, action of the ears, lips, &c., indicate clearly the intentions, dictating the hazard to be incurred. Whatever may be the feelings, great boldness of expression and action is indispensable. This not only aids in keeping resistance in check, but, under some circumstances, may be the means of preserving life. The control of horses is like that of an intricate but powerful machine, when under the subjection of skillful management. If horses be subjected to skillful and prudent management, they will easily be made docile and controlable; on the other hand, subjected to rude, imprudent treatment, they are at once liable to become unreliable, hostile and impulsive brutes. The generous reward of this skill should be an incentive to every one to acquire a correct knowledge of their duty.

That there is great loss of life, and many lamentable accidents, almost daily, in every neighborhood, from the use of horses that are dangerously vicious and unmanageable, cannot be questioned.

One horse will run away, if given the least freedom; another is liable to kick himself clear from the wagon, if a strap dangle against his flanks, or if the breech break, or anything of the kind occurs to excite his fear. One horse will balk, another goes when and where he pleases, generally pleasing to go any way but the right one; another cannot be harnessed with safety; another will kick, if the rein touches his hip, or is caught under his tail; one will not stand while being mounted, or while getting into the carriage; another will not back; others are frightened, and sheer and jump at sight of a stone, stump or paper in the street; while to others an umbrella, railroad track or buffalo robe are objects of fear. There are but a very few horses which are considered *well broken* that have not some habits that lessen their value.

It is seen how easily I make the worst of horses yield to my control; and if my instructions are thoroughly practised, success must inevitably be the result. As I have heretofore said, the great secret of training horses, is first to get control of them. This must be done by fear. They must be taught that you can and will be their master. Nothing in this regard is so effective as *throwing* the horse. This has been allowed for years by all successful horsemen who have preceded me.

The first subject to which I invite your attention is the young, green colt. "Teach him in his youth the way he should go, and when he is old he will not depart from it."

We must not permit the colt or filly to go wild and run riot until it shall have attained its full strength, its full energies, and the full sway of its natural temper unrestrained, without making an effort to train or teach it until it be two or three years old, then take it up, and saddle and bridle it by force, and putting it into the hands of some fearless, hard-hearted, mutton-fisted, rough-riding fellow, scarcely less a brute in all points of humanity than that which he professes to teach, expect it to be turned out, by dint of whip and spurs, a gentle animal, rendered so by brute violence. The education of a colt can hardly commence too early. He should be handled frequently by different persons, and should be made accustomed to whatever is likely to attract his attention when he is put in harness.

The more he is accustomed to straps, the less likely will he be to become frightened by accidental breaking of the harness, by the falling of a trace about his heels, or by having the reins thrown about his back by a careless driver.

Young horses, while mere foals, nursing by their mothers' sides, should be accustomed to be fearless; to feed from the hand, to suffer themselves to be handled, to have their feet handled, lifted and tapped with the hands or a hammer on the soles; to be led to and fro by the forelock; to endure pressure of the hand on the back; to rejoice in being flattered, caressed and spoken to. They should be very early equipped with a head-stall, having a ring appended, to which a holder can be attached, and by these means they can be easily taught to follow at any pace; the person leading them may adopt walking, running or stopping, as he may desire. Punishment at this period should never be resorted to, but rewards should be continually offered. Carry in your pockets bits of sugar, or apples, and give to the little creature with a caress, when it has done what is required of it,

Soon after this a pad may be strapped on the back for a few hours daily, and after a time stirrup leathers, the stirrups appended to them, may be suffered to play about, by which means all fear of such things will be removed long enough before it will become necessary to saddle him for any real purpose. When he is about a year old, the colt's bits should be occasionally put in his mouth, and he should be reined up gently to the surcingle, and allowed to play with them, or mouth them; after this he may stand for an hour or two between the pillars with the rein attached from the colt's bit to rings placed at a proper height in the standards. But here it it is necessary to observe, above almost anything in the world, that it is fatal to the formation of the animal's mouth to place the rings too high, or to bear up the head above its ordinary and natural elevation. This is often done to give a lofty carriage to the colt's head, and produce a proud bearing. It does nothing of the kind. It causes the horse, weary with having its head forced into an unnatural position, to bear, to weigh, to hang upon the bits,—to become accustomed to their pressure, and to find pleasure instead of pain from it, so that, at last, it acquires a mouth perfectly unimpressive and muscles set and rigid.

Shortly after this the colt should be walked in a circle, with a long cord attached to the breaking-bits, in a smooth grass field, by which means he is taught his paces, taught to regulate them, taught to moderate, to increase or diminish his speed, to change his leg, to come toward the operator, or to stop dead short at a signal either of the voice or crack of the whip. For this it requires only time, patience and good temper to effect, and when effected, half the business is done.

No attempt should be made to put the colt to work before he is three and a half or four years old, and it would be far better to exact no work, beyond what is necessary for gentle exercise, before he is six years old; this, although not at first remunerative, is eminently so in the end; for the two years lost in early life will generally add six or eight years to a horse's working time. A colt, educated according to the preceding remarks, will not need the treatment contained in the next chapter; but as all colts are not educated when young, it is necessary that I give a method by which they can be brought under perfect control.

THE COLT AND HIS MANAGEMENT.

The first step to be taken is to see that the lot or yard in which you intend to handle him, is clear from all obstacles which might injure him or serve to attract his attention; as it is natural for a colt to be attracted by all domestic animals, they should be driven from the enclosure, also all persons except the one undertaking his management. This precaution should be taken for two reasons: first, they would attract his attention and direct his mind from you; and, secondly, by permitting the presence of any one not a member of my class you would violate your contract

TO HALTER-BREAK A WILD COLT

THE first object being to halter the colt. If he is not very wild, you can easily do this by working up to the head; by scratching the neck slip the halter on the head. Should he seem vicious, this may be difficult, if not dangerous to do, and one of the most important requisites is to guard against injury either to yourself or the horse, and at the same time to accomplish your work most easily and surely. Your best way of procedure is as follows:

Take a small pole, ten to fifteen feet long, more or less as you may find it necessary to safety; drive an eight-penny nail three to four inches from the end into the stick, and another nail from ten to twelve inches from the first one; take a common rope halter with a running-noose, pull the part that slips through the noose back about one foot, then hang the part that goes over the head upon the nails, with the hitching-part held in your hands with the pole; your halter is now so opened and hung on the nails as to be easily placed upon the head. If the colt is not too much excited, he is easily attracted to notice anything new to him; he has no way of examining objects but by his nose, and so he is prompted to smell and feel of things, consequently you will find upon holding out the halter gently, hung (as above) upon the end of the pole, he will reach out to smell of it, and while he is gratifying his curiosity in this way you can easily raise the stick high enough to bring the halter over and back of the ears, when, by turning the stick around, the halter will drop from it upon the head. This may startle him some, and cause him to run from you; but by doing so the slack of the halter, passing under the jaw through the noose, will draw up and the halter is on the head safely. Your colt now being haltered, your next object is to teach him to submit to its restraint. Stand about on a line with the shoulder, but some distance from him, and give a sharp, quick pull towards you, but instantly slack up on the halter. You have the greatest advantage from this position, and by adroitly following up this advantage, not attempting to pull upon the colt when he attempts to run back from you, he will soon, by a few sharp pulls in this way, learn to feel and submit to the force of your power.

As soon as he will permit you to approach and unloose the noose from his neck, using kind words, caress and let him know you do not wish to hurt him; continue to caress him till he will permit you to rub his neck and ears, and encourage him by feeding apples and sugar from your hand.

When he submits so far as to let you handle his head, put on him the Bonaparte or Camanche bridle, made in the following manner:

You should have the best manilla three thread rope, made small and strong; of this take 16 feet, tie a hard knot in one end of it, and a loose knot far enough from the end

BRIDLES.

to reach around the colt's neck; pass the hard knot through the loose one, draw it up tight, tuck the middle of the rope under the one around the neck, making a loop, which you pass up through the mouth, keeping the end of the rope in your hand. A green colt is not bad about taking anything in his mouth if judgment is used, and you do not frighten him; slip the loop up well over the jaws under the roof of his mouth, draw up on the loop, and take off the halter you first had around his neck. By taking hold of the end of the cord you will find you now have a means of power in your hands, which will enable you to control the strongest animal with ease and safety, and I believe the Bonaparte bridle, and its value in managing and training colts, cannot be over-estimated when used with judgment, and handled with adroitness and skill.

It should never be used so harshly as to excite extreme pain, and yet with a touch that causes fear of resistance. If he should endeavor to run away from you give him a quick, sharp jerk, and at the same time say "ho!" always giving him the command before jerking on the cord. Repeat this treatment as often as he may make the attempt to get away; when he stops, go up to him and caress him about the head; when he gives up to the rope enough, so that he does not try to get away, proceed to teach him to lead. With your rope in hand, step back to his side, opposite his hips, and say, come here! at the same time give him a quick, sharp pull with the halter; he will swing round towards you, and if he only takes one step in the right direction, show him by a caress that he has done what you desired of him. Continue to ca ress him for every step taken in the right direction, and he will very soon learn to follow you at the word.

If the colt is willful and stubborn, handle him with the Camanche bridle until he will stand quietly, then take your strap (previously provided) in the right hand, holding by the buckle, commence raising the foot next to you. If he resists your efforts reprove him with the halter. Continue your efforts till you can take the foot in your hand, then slip the strap around below the fetlock; putting the end through the keeper on the inside of the buckle, draw it up tight, so it will not slip up, then pass the strap through between the horse and surcingle, and fasten it to the surcingle by buckling.

By putting him on three legs, he can offer but slight resistance when pulled by the head sidewise, and will come around as readily with his legs free as he will with one strapped up. Step back on a line with the hips, holding the halter firmly in your hand, and say, come here! He, of course, does not come, so you pull on the bridle, and he is obliged to swing around to you. Step around to the other side and repeat, bring him around by the halter each time, till when he hears the words, come here, he will obey readily. As soon as the colt submits to this step, remove the strap from his leg and rub the foot gently where the strap has been. Step back, and, as before, say, come here! If he does not come readily, give him a sharp, quick pull with the rope, which shows him you can handle him as well on four legs as on three; continue to caress him for every step forward till he follows readily.

HOW TO BIT A COLT, AND MAKE A BRIDLE.

(See Engraving, page 37.)

THE object aimed at in bitting a horse is to give an easy position, with a a high and graceful carriage of the head; and, in our efforts to do this, we must be carêful not to give him a dead bearing on the bit, or make him what is usually known as a lugger. All the bitting rigs which we have examined, and especially those of English make, are objectionable, as having a a tendency to produce this result. The rig which we here give you is entirely free from this objection, and is better calculated to produce the desired result of ease and gracefulness, than any ever before presented to the public. Our rig, instead of bearing on the jawbones, whenever the horse presses his weight upon the bit, producing a caloused jaw and indifference to the bit, contracts the side muscles of the cheeks on the molar teeth with a pain the horse cannot endure; he lifts his head, the bit falls on the side-rein, and the mouth is at once relieved. Practice has shown that horses bitted with this rig soon acquire the habit of gently and gracefully raising the head, with that occasional toss, or upward and downward motion, and playing with the bit, which is the perfection of beauty in a carriage horse, while standing in the harness.

It is not possible for a horse with our rig to become a "lugger;" this bit never bears upon the jawbone with more than a light pressure, and when he attempts to rest his head upon the bit, the pressure on the teeth causes him to desist and elevate his head. He soon dreads to rest upon the bit, and of his own free will, without the force of the rein, carries it up with freedom and ease.

COLT WEARING OUR BITTING RIG.

OUR mode of bitting a colt, is to **put** on him our bridle without reins, and turn him loose. Do this a few times until he is familiarized with the bit, which should be large, say an inch in diameter at the end, and tapering to half an inch at the joint, and short—not more than five inches—between the crossbars; it should also have a tongue-plate and drops. The crossbars should be stout, and six inches long, the rings two inches in diameter, and the whole bit well plated or tinned.

Take a gag-runner bridle, without blinders, put in the bit I have described, if one can be had, if not, get a jointed bit as nearly like it as you can. Fasten to the head part of the bridle either a leather strap, or a common bed-cord; pass it down through the bit, and up through the gag-runners; let it be long enough to pass back to, and a little beyond, the girth. Take a common surcingle, fasten pads to the back to prevent its turning, put on it three loops of leather—one at the centre of the back, and one on each side. The one on the back should be lengthwise of the surcingle, with a space about two inches long, and so that when the girth is buckled, you can freely pass your three fingers into it. Those on the side should be put on double, like bootstraps. Make the loops an inch and a half or two inches long; get a common crupper and back-strap; let the centre of the gag-reins be passed through the loop on the back; they will show a loop behind the girth, into which fasten the back-strap from the crupper, so that you can tighten and elevate the head as wanted. Then take two other cords; fasten one end of each to the crupper, pass one down on each side, through the loop on the girth, and tie the end into the ring of the bridle-bit. The manner in which it is put on and worn is shown in figure given above, the colt being very gently reined in.

BREAKING COLTS TO HARNESS.

PUT on your harness carefully, after first having it made to fit well, being made strong and safe in every part. Never, on any account, drive a colt in an unsafe harness, or before a vehicle liable to break down. As many of the bad habits horses have are the result of imprudent proccedings. After applying the harness, allow the colt to stand in his stall, or walk about the yard for half or three-quarters of an hour, till he becomes used to the pressure of the different parts, and does not notice the rattling, or care for its presence. As soon as he seems perfectly quiet, check him up loosely, and drive him about the yard. So soon as he becomes familiar with the check and reins, and will stop and start at the word, and drive to the right and left, it is safe to drive him in the street; always putting on the Camanche or Bonaparte bridle for safety. I consider a sulky preferable at first. Let the colt smell and examine every part, to show him it is not an object of fear; draw it up behind him, rattling and running it back and forth before attaching the harness. Before starting him, back him up against the cross-bar of the shafts. In case he acts frightened, speak calmly and firmly, at the same time holding the reins tight, to prevent him from swinging around, should he be so disposed. Then go up to him and caress him till he is again quiet. Then run the sulky against his haunches, at the same time soothing him by kind words till you can push the sulky about him as you please, and he care nothing about it. You can then take your seat in the vehicle, and drive him wherever you choose without danger. Let him go slowly at first, to become familiar with the objects along the road liable to cause fear.

OBJECTS OF FEAR.

IN driving, be careful not to make too free use of the whip. If objects which you are obliged to pass are regarded by the horse with fear, never urge him to pass them fast, or excite him by using the whip. Let him stand and look at the object, and drive him as close as convenient, allowing him to smell of it, and see that no harm is intended him; at the same time talk encouragingly to him, and, in this manner, he will soon be fearless and confident, as well as regardless of such things. Should you, on the other hand, whip him for becoming frightened at such things, he will be apt to associate the punishment with the object of fear, and be more frightened the next time he sees it.

TO RECONCILE THE COLT TO A ROBE.

FIRST, while under careful restraint (by the use of the war-bridle), let the robe be brought up gently to the colt's nose. After permitting him to feel and smell of it till satisfied it is harmless, rub it gently against his head, neck and body, the way the hair lies, as he will permit. Then, stepping off a short distance, throw it across his back, and over the neck and head, till you can throw the robe around him anywhere, and it is no longer an object of fear.

TO OVERCOME THE FEAR OF AN UMBRELLA.

WHILE holding the colt, as before, with the bridle, bring the umbrella towards him, and allow him to smell of it a little; rub it against his head and body, spread it a little, and continue to caress him till you can raise it over his head, and pass it around him as you please, without exciting fear. This same proceeding is applicable under all circumstances. Even as it is said that "familiarity breeds contempt," it may be said of the colt in regard to objects of fear. Let him approach near enough to the dreaded article, and he ignores the idea of being afraid of it. In order to make the colt familiar with the cars, he should be led to them often, and permitted to remain about them. At first, when they are not in motion, and then again when they are moving. In this way continue till he is familiar with them. In any event, do not fail to repeat your lessons till your object is attained.

TEACHING THE COLT TO BACK.

WHEN the colt drives well to the reins, he should be taught to back. This brings in use again the Camanche bridle. Should he act stubbornly, after using it a few moments, reverse, by putting the large loop over his neck, which will touch him more sharply. If the colt should become warm after a lesson of five or ten minutes, stop; and repeat the lesson any time after he becomes cool and quiet. The colt will soon learn to back promptly. You may now put on reins, and teach him to back by being pulled upon from behind. The lesson should be repeated till the colt is prompt in his obedience. He may now be backed to a wagon, but at first on a slightly descending grade, gradually requiring more of him till he will obey promptly.

The same is applicable in teaching a colt to draw a load. You can gradually increase the amount, till he will draw to the extent of his ability, without comprehending that he has power to do otherwise.

After your horse is educated to the use of the harness, you may either allow him to carry his head as nature may dictate, or by the use of the check-rein bring his neck into such position of style as you may fancy. I once heard a friend say that he tamed a very young colt to step upon a shelf or box (arranged about a foot above the stable floor), with his fore-feet, and reach for and eat his oats from a box, placed high enough, so that he must stretch his neck, and bend down his head to procure his food. This, practised three times each day, while he was growing fast, gave a natural curve to his neck, making him much admired, and of more than ordinary value, by one hundred dollars. These little ideas, if carried into practice, will repay one for their time and trouble, by making an otherwise ordinary looking colt give an imposing appearance, to gratify the pride of his owner, as well as bring an advanced price when a sale is desirable. It is a true maxim: "As the twig is bent, so is the tree inclined."

TREATMENT OF VICIOUS HORSES.

IT it my desire throughout this book to impress it upon the reader's mind that colts are not naturally vicious, and horses are only so through mismanagement when colts. I must now proceed to teach you how to conquer vicious horses, and cure them of their faults. This is an easy matter, though requiring time, perseverance and patience. I have never failed to cure the worst of horses in a short space of time, in from one to three lessons, according to the degree of their viciousness.

FOR BALKY HORSES.

THIS habit tries the patience of man more than any other, yet by patience and tact it may be broken up. Horses with this habit are usually high-spirited, and of a nervous temperament. They resist, because we have failed to make them understand what we require of them, or it may be from a sore shoulder. Over-loading, or working till tired out, is particularly the cause with young animals. The whip, under such circumstances, only excites them to more determined resistance. On the first attempt of your horse to balk, get out of the wagon, pat him on the neck, examine the harness carefully, first on one side, then on the other. Encourage him, at the same time, with kind words, and again reseat yourself in your vehicle, and give the word, go; generally he will obey. If he is still obstinate, take him from the carriage, put up the traces, so they will not drag on the ground, take him by the head and tail, reel him around till almost ready to fall. This seldom fails to bring about the desired result. By repeating this lesson each day for a week, this most perplexing habit will be thoroughly and lastingly broken up.

Another method, advisable to break a

balky horse in double harness is, to take a hemp cord, pass around under the tail, bring forward through the terret-ring of the balky horse, and fasten to the other horse's hame. Thus when he starts, the balky one can do no other way than to move with him, and, in a short time, if he is hitched single or double, by taking your whip or common stick, and put on the back of the crupper-strap, the horse will start readily.

In the following chapter I will explain how I throw a horse, making him lie down quietly, and almost as easily as when by himself in the stall. It can be done with perfect safety, and whatever may be the vice to which your horse is addicted, it is a good plan to give him a course of training, by throwing, and handling him just as you please, when down; demonstrating to him that it is worse than useless to resist control. It is also the best way to handle and manage nervous horses I have ever tried. After having been handled gently, when down, their fear passes away, and you can do with them just as you please.

HOW TO THROW THE HORSE.

PLACE upon the animal a strong surcingle, about three inches back of the fore legs; connected with this must be a strong crupper. There must be a strong ring, about one inch in diameter, at the top of the surcingle, or rope in the centre of the back, and another one upon the right side, in the centre. This being adjusted, proceed to strap up the left fore-leg as follows. (*See Engraving.*) Take a common quarter-strap, pass it two or three times around the leg, between the coffin and postern-joints, and then buckle the leg close up to the belly. Place around the horse's neck a quarter-inch rope (or three-eighths) loosely, fixing the knot so it will not slip; bring the end down the near side of the head, through the mouth, and back on the off-side, through either of the rings in the surcingle. The one in the centre of the side, if the first

time throwing, will give you greater control, with less exertion. Upon pulling on the rope, standing in my position, the horse must come upon his side, and without injury.

In practice, all will perceive the decided advantage of this over any other system. The operation must be repeated from ten to twenty times, or until the horse seems entirely *disgusted* with the controversy. This operation, if properly conducted, will result in obtaining control of the horse, and in his willingness to be accommodating at least. The next thing is to teach him the meaning of the word, *whoa!* and to obey it when spoken to him as a command. This also breaks him to the bridle. Place in his mouth the scissors or **W** bit, with head-stall and lines attached (an ordinary bit will do, though the one named is preferable, as being more secure); now let the horse walk off a few feet, twelve or twenty, and all at once jerk with all your force, accompanying the action with the word "whoa!" When he stops, step to his side and caress him. This, repeated eight or ten times, will teach the horse lastingly the word and its meaning. You must say, "whoa!" just before you pull. This treatment of the horse must be repeated, if at any time he grows restive, and seems indisposed to obey the command. Sometimes an occasional jerk preceded by the command, with an ordinary bit, is sufficient to refresh his memory on the subject. This method is also effectual in breaking up the habit of kicking. For this habit I sometimes use a link bit, never before presented to the public. It is made of six links, each link one inch in length, making a chain nearly six inches long. Place at each end of this a 2½ inch ring (*See Engraving of Kicking Rig*). With the aid of this treatment you can cure the worst of kickers, and horses in the habit of running away can usually be cured in one lesson, thus preventing accidents for the future. It is by this process of teaching that horses are driven without head-stall or bridle.

TO CURE A HALTER PULLER.

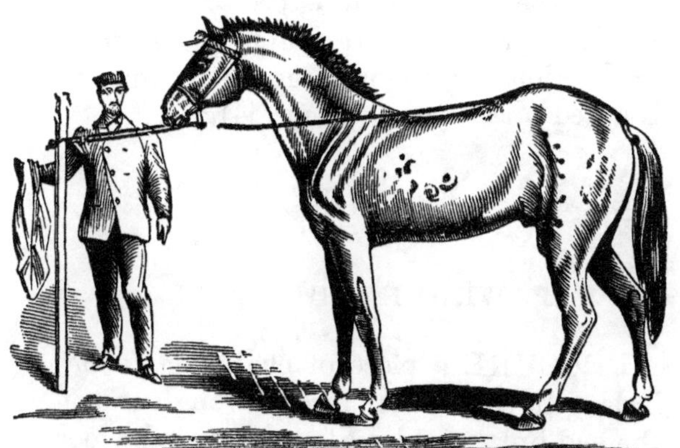

PLACE on him a common head-stall, put on him a girth, take a quarter-inch rope, sixteen feet long; pass the centre of this rope under his tail in place of a crupper, twist this rope over a couple of times, pass the ends under the girth upon each side of the neck, and then through the noose piece of the head-stall under the check piece (*See Engraving*), and tie to a strong post, leaving three feet play of the rope. Strike him with a bag. As soon as the horse pulls back, he being tied by the tail to the post, the hurt comes there, and not on the head, as he expected; he starts up. For this you caress him, and if these instructions are followed up a few times he is cured (*See engraving page* 54).

PAWING IN THE STALL.

PROCURE a piece of chain ten inches in length, run a short strap through one of the end links, and buckle it around the foot above the fetlock. When the horse attempts to paw or kick, the chain rattles against the the foot, and prevents a repetition of the practice.

A NEW METHOD OF BREAKING A KICKER.

THROW the horse (according to direction previously given) from ten to twenty times, till he is quiet; strike him lightly with your foot, when down, below where the breeching comes, to tame him, and cure him of being afraid to be touched around the hind parts. Then let him up, and back him into the two-wheeled rig. If he still continues to kick, put on the kicking rig, as shown in the engraving.

When this rig is put on, it punishes the horse in the mouth, thus diverting his attention from his heels.

First, attach a rope to the bridle-bit ring on the near side, then pass it over the head through the off-bit ring, then down between his fore legs, through under the belly-band, and fasten to a pulley. Attach another rope to the off bridle-bit ring, over the head through the near side-bit ring; then pass it between the fore legs to the pulley, and fasten. Now, put on straps above and below the gambol joint on each hind leg, with a ring in the straps. Attach a rope to the ring on the near hind leg, and pass it through the pulley to the off hind leg, thus allowing the horse to walk or trot in a natural position.

TO HARDEN A TENDER-MOUTHED HORSE.

PLACE the bits in the animal's mouth as low as possible, not to have them drop out, and drive him from two to three weeks with the bits in this way, and when they are buckled up in proper place he is hard-mouthed.

LOLLING THE TONGUE.

SOME horses have the habit of carrying the tongue out of the side of the mouth. This is generally confined to a narrow-jawed horse. The space between the molar teeth being too narrow to contain the tongue in the mouth when the bit presses upon it, without coming in contact with the edges of the molar teeth. To prevent this the tongue is thrown out over the bit, and hangs from one side of the mouth. To remedy this defect, take a common bar-bit, and drill a hole on either side, about three-quarters of an inch from the centre of the upper surface of the bit; then take a piece of sole leather, four inches long and two inches wide, sprinkle it over with rosin and burn it into the leather. This renders it proof against the action of the saliva in the mouth. Drill two holes in the centre of the leather, corresponding with those in the bit, and secure both together by rivets, so that the leather extends two inches above the bit, and two inches below it. This, put in the mouth, keeps the tongue down clear of the molar teeth, and prevents the animal getting it over the bit.

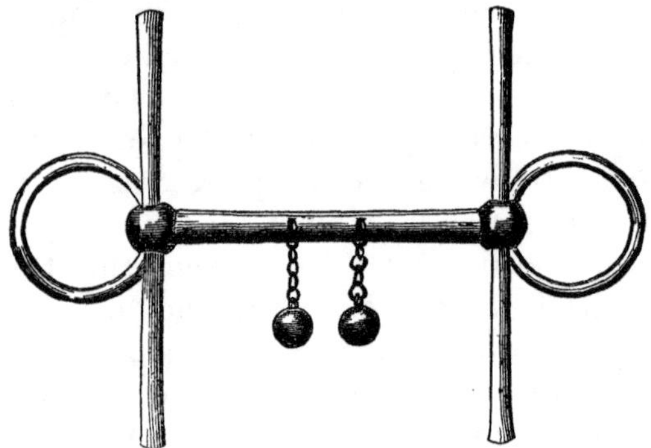

Another way to cure a horse of lolling the tongue. Place on him the bit shown in the above cut, and let it remain on him from 4 to 6 weeks.

HUGGING THE POLE.

THIS is a great annoyance to the other horse, and he will probably learn to do the same thing, not from imitation, but from leaning inwards, so as to enable him to stand against the other horse, leaning upon him. This habit may be broken up by securing a piece of sole leather to the pole upon the side where the animal leans, having a number of tacks driven through it in such a manner as to protrude from the leather towards the horse.

UGLY TO BRIDLE.

SOME horses are ugly to bridle, from having been knocked, or roughly handled about the head. Horses are occasionally troubled with tender ears, and have some tenderness about the mouth; such animals refuse to be bridled from fear of being hurt; nothing but kindness and careful handling will accomplish our purpose. In such cases, where the habit arises from previous injuries, or from ugliness of disposition, take a cord, put the end in the mouth, draw it tightly and take a half-hitch; this confines the head and prevents the animal from raising it. In this position the horse will allow you to put on and take off the bridle at pleasure. After putting it on, remove it several times, unloose the cord and repeat the bridling. Every time the animal resists, draw the cord tightly. On the contrary, when he yields, caress him, you thus gain his confidence.

LUGGERS ON THE BIT,

BUCKLE a pair of straps, about twelve inches long, with a ring at one end, and a buckle at the other, to the check-piece, and let the straps pass through the rings on either side of the bit; buckle the lines to the rings on these straps, instead of the rings on the bit; this forms a gag similar to the French twitch gag, and is a powerful means of controlling the mouth of a hard-pulling horse.

THE JUMPING RIG. .

BUCKLE a strap to the fore legs, below

the knees; pass it up under a surcingle, previously placed around the body; attach the other cords to rings connecting two straps, one above and one below the gambol joints. When rearing to go over the fence it will take his hind feet from under him, and set him back in the field where he started from.

TO CURE A CRIBBER.

CUT a strip of sheepskin with long wool, about eight inches wide, and long enough to cover the front edge of the manger, and tie the horse in the stall, so he cannot crib anywhere except on the sheepskin. If this does not cure him, sprinkle on a little cayenne pepper. Another remedy is to take a wooden roller, long enough to reach across the stall; let the horse eat his hay and grain from the bottom of the manger, when he attempts to crib he must inevitably work on the roller, which, when he places his teeth to crib, the roller turns, his lips come in contact with the roller, and he is punished at every attempt, and, after a few trials, becomes satisfied, and will not again attempt to crib.

TO LEAD A HORSE BEHIND A WAGON.

TAKE a stout cord, or small rope, and place under his tail; cross on the back, and run through the rings of the halter; first hitch him to a post, and by hitting him over the nose with something to excite him, make him pull, which will satisfy him of his useless attempts at holding back on the halter. You may then hitch him to the wagon, and you will find no further trouble in leading him.

TO BREAK A HORSE OF KICKING AT ITS MATE IN A STALL.

PUT on the Bonaparte bridle, with the small loop on the lower jaw, letting the cord pass back to the hind leg. Attach it to a small ring, fastened around the leg, with two hame straps above and below the gambol joint.

TO BREAK A HORSE OF KICKING AT PERSONS ENTERING THE STALL.

PUT on the Bonaparte bridle, making a loop around the lower jaw; pass it up over the head, and down through the loop on the jaw. Run the cord through a small ring, fastened by means of a staple, to the side of the stall, a little back of the horse's head. Pass the cord back to another ring fastened in the side of the front of the stall. When you enter the stall pull on this rope, and, at the same time, say, "go over." The head of the horse will be thus drawn towards you, and his heels *must* go to the other side of the stall. Most horses will be broken of this very dangerous habit in two or three lessons.

TO PREVENT A HORSE FROM GETTING CAST IN THE STALL.

FASTEN a little pulley at the side of the stall, near the ceiling, and over the manger. Pass a small cord through the pulley, and to the end attach a weight of one pound. In the centre of the stall drive a ring and staple in the ceiling; pass the other end of the cord through the ring, and attach it to the horse's head, giving him oats on the floor; draw the cord tight, and tie it to a small ring fastened in the top of the halter for this purpose. The horse can now lie down, but cannot get the top of his head to the floor, and if he cannot get the top of his head to the floor, he cannot roll, and if he cannot roll, he cannot get cast.

A HORSE BAD TO SHOE.

THE habit of resistance to being shod, or allowing the feet to be handled, like all others to which horses are subject, is the result of careless and imprudent management. It would seem, from the reckless disregard of consequences so generally evinced in handling young horses, as though man doubted his own reason, and would not take counsel of the teachings of prudence. If the feet had been handled gently at first (as I have directed), and blacksmiths had not vented so much of their impatience in the way of pounding with the hammer for every little movement or resistance in shoeing, this habit would never have been contracted. The natural tractability of the horse causes him to yield a ready obedience to all reasonable demands, that he comprehends. If the feet are jerked up roughly, and without an effort to reconcile him to being handled, the colt will strive to get away, or free himself from what he supposes will hurt him. Never hold to the foot with all your might, when the colt is trying to jerk away, for, in such a case, strength is not your forte, and your struggles only convince the horse of your weakness. Handle the horse in conformity with the laws of his nature, so as not to excite resistance through fear of injury. If the horse does not very much resist the handling of his feet, put the Camanche bridle on him, and put a short strap on his hind foot. Pulling upon the strap will bring the foot forward, and he will probably resist by kicking. The instant he kicks, reprove him with the bridle, which is held in the other hand, and so continue until the foot can be held without resistance. But, if your subject is very bad, take a strap or rope, about twelve feet long, and tie one end of it in a loop around his neck, where the collar rests; pass the other end back between the fore legs, and around the near hind leg, below the fetlock, thence back between the legs, and through the loop around the neck. Now step in front of the horse, and take a firm hold of the rope or strap, and give a quick pull on it, which will bring the foot forward; pull the foot as far forward as you can, which will give you the more advantage. The horse will try to free the foot by kicking. Hold the head firmly with the left hand, and with the other hold the strap firmly. Stand right up to the horse's shoulder, and whirl him about you, which you can easily do while he struggles to free himself. As soon as he yields, handle the foot gently, and then let up on it a little, and so continue till he will let you handle the foot without resistance. It may be necessary to repeat the lesson once or twice, and be careful to handle the foot with the greatest gentleness. If the rope is rough, put a collar on the neck instead of the loop, and fasten your strap to it. Use a smooth, soft strap, so as not to chafe the foot where it passes around it.

SHOEING.

IF we examine the horse's feet in their natural state, they will be found to be almost round and very elastic at the heel, the frog broad, plump, and of a soft, yielding nature; the commissures open and well defined, the sole concave, the outside crust from the heel to the toe increased from a slight bevel to an angle of forty-five degrees; consequently, as the foot grows, it becomes wider and longer in proportion to the amount of horn secreted, and narrower and shorter in proportion to the ground-surface. If a shoe were fitted nicely and accurately to the foot after being dressed down well, it would be found too narrow and short for the same foot, after the lapse of a few weeks. If any unyielding shoe of iron is nailed firmly to this naturally enlarging and elastic hoof, it prevents its natural freedom of expansion almost wholly, and does not allow the foot to grow wider at the quarters as it grows down, in proportion to the amount of horn grown as before shod; consequently the foot is changed by the continued restraint of the shoe, from a nearly round, healthy foot, to a contracted and unhealthy condition, as generally seen in horses shod for a few years.

The principles which govern in shoeing are few and simple, and it is surprising, considering the serious results involved, that it should be done with so little consideration. The object of the shoer, in trimming and preparing the hoof for the shoe, should be to keep the foot natural, and this involves, first, the cutting away of any undue accumulation of horn, affecting in the least its health and freedom; second, to carry out in the shape of the shoe that of the foot, as nearly as possible; third, to fit and fasten the shoe to the foot, so as least to interfere with its health, growth, and elasticity.

The preparation of the foot requires the cutting away of about the proportion of horn, which, coming in contact with the ground, would have worn off, or which has accumulated since being last shod; if the shoes have been on a month, the proportion of horn secreted in that time is to be removed; if two months, then the proportion of two months' growth. No definite rule can be given, the judgment must be governed by the circumstances of the case; the stronger and more rapid the growth of the foot, the more must be cut away; and the weaker and the less horn produced, the less, to the extent of simply leveling the crust a little, the better to conform to the shoe; there is generally a far more rapid growth of horn at the toe than at the heels or quarters; more will be required to be taken off there than of the other parts; therefore shorten the toe, and lower the heels, until you succeed in bringing down the bearing-surface of the hoof upon the shoe to almost a level with the live-horn of the sole. Be careful to make the heels level; having lowered the crust to the necessary extent, smooth it down level with the rasp, the sole and frog detach by exfoliation, as it becomes superabundant. The sole would not need paring, were it not for the restraining effect of the shoe upon the general function of the foot, which is liable to prevent such detachment of the horn. The cutting away of the bars to give the heels an open appearance is inexcusable, and should never be done. In a natural healthy condition, the frog has a line of bearing with the hoof, and by its elastic nature acts as a safeguard to the delicate machinery of the foot immediately over it, and helps to preserve the foot in its natural state, by keeping the heel spread. It seems to be wisely intended to give life and health to the foot. Permitting the heels to grow down, with the addition of high-heeled shoes, raises the frog from its natural position, and causes it to shrink and harden; and bears, in consequence, an important influence in setting up a diseased action, that usually results in contraction of the foot. If the heels are square and high, and the hoof presents rather a long, narrow appearance, and is hollow on the bottom, there is a state of contraction going on, and you must not hesitate to dress down thoroughly. Do not hesitate because the hoof appears small. Cut away until you are well down to a level with the live-horn of the sole, and if the foot is weak, use the same prudence in not cutting it away too much. The shoer must always bear in mind that the sole must not rest on the shoe. Let the foot be so dressed down, and the shoe so approximate, that the bearing will come evenly upon the crust all the way around, without the sole touching the shoe. This requires the crust to be dressed down level, and, although well down to the live-horn of the sole, it should always be left a little higher. The corners between the bars and crust should be well pared out, so there is no danger of the sole resting on the shoe, which is our next consideration.

THE SHOE.

THE main object should be to have the shoe so formed as to size, weight, fitting, and fastening, as to combine the most advantages of protection, and preserve the natural tread of the foot the best. In weight, it should be proportioned to the work or employment of the horse. The foot should not be loaded with more iron than is necessary to preserve it. If the work of the horse is principally on the road, at heavy draught, the shoe should be rather heavy, in order that it may not be bent by contact with hard, uneven earth; it should be wide in the web, and of equal thickness and width from the toe to the heel, that it may as much as possible protect the sole, without altering the natural position of the foot; it should be well drawn in at the heels, that it may rest on the bars, thereby protecting the corn place, or angles between the bar and crust, and should in no part extend beyond the outer edge of the crust.

It is too often the case that the shoe is made according to the smith's notions of what the form of the horse's foot should be, and the foot is pared, burned, and rasped until it fits the shoe. Now, it should always be borne in mind that the shoe is intended for the foot, and not the foot for the shoe, and that it is therefore peculiarly proper to make the shoe fit the natural form of the foot. It is impossible to have the foot of a horse sound and safe, for work and use, after bringing it to an unnatural figure, by the use of the knife and rasp. The foot of the horse being elastic, it expands to the weight of the horse, in precisely the same degree, whether resting upon the most open or the most contracted shoe. Therefore, the shape of the shoe cannot possibly affect the shape of the foot. The form of the foot is determined by the situation of the nails. If the nails are placed so that the inside quarters and heels are left free to expand in a natural manner, no shape which we can give to the shoe can of itself change the form of the foot. It must not be inferred, however, from this that the shape of the shoe is of no importance; quite the contrary being the case, as I have already shown. In forming the shoe, we should always adopt that which produces the greatest number of advantages with the fewest disadvantages.

We find that the sole-surface of the foot is by nature concave in form, which seems to offer the greatest fulcrum of resistance to the horse when travelling. It is important to preserve the natural mechanical action of the horn and sole; therefore the ground surface of the foot, that is to say, the ground surface of the shoe, should be leveled cup fashion; its outer edge being prominent, corresponds to the lower and outer rim of the hoof; while the shoe being hollow, resembles the natural cavity of the sole of the foot. The ground surface of the shoe should always be concave.

The pattern that nature has presented us in making the sole concave, cannot be improved upon by the smith, with all his skill. The expansion of the heels, and growth of the foot, require that the shoe should be long enough, and wide enough at the heels, to allow for the natural growth of the foot in the time it is calculated the shoe should be on before being reset; for as the foot enlarges, the shoe is brought forward until it loses its original proportion, and becomes too short and narrow. The shoe may be about a quarter of an inch wider and longer than the extreme bearing of the heels; and the nail holes should be punched coarse and in the centre of the web. The manner of fastening the shoe is what really affects the foot, and what requires the most special attention in shoeing; for the foot, being elastic, expands in the same proportion on the rough as on the nicely-fitted shoe. It is the number and position of the nails that really affect the foot. If they are placed well back in the quarters, four on a side, as is common, the crust is held as firmly to this unyielding shoe as if in a vice, which utterly prevents the free action necessary to its health. Inflammation is produced, which causes contraction and the consequent derangement of the whole foot. If the free, natural expansion of the foot, and the spreading of the quarters in proportion to the growth of the hoof is prevented by the nailing of the shoe, irritation of the fleshy substance between the crust and coffin-bone will result, and ultimately create so much diseased action of the parts as to cause contraction and nervicular disease. Shoes may be fastened without causing such mischief, if the following method of nailing is observed.

In experimenting, for the purpose of ascertaining how few nails are absolutely necessary, under ordinary circumstances, for retaining the shoe securely in its place as long as it should remain upon the foot, it has been satisfactorily established that five nails are amply sufficient for the fore shoes, and seven for the hind ones, three should be placed on the outside of the foot, and two on the inner side, near the toe, thereby leaving the foot free to expand in a natural manner. The nails should not be driven high up in the crust, but brought out as soon as possible. Another mistake with most smiths is in rasping the clinches away too fine; they should be turned broad and flat. It is also a custom with some to rasp and sandpaper the whole surface of the hoof, for the purpose of making it look nice and smooth. Such a practice should never be tolerated, the covering thus removed is provided by nature to protect the too rapid evaporation of the moisture of the hoof, and when taken away, causes the horn to become dry and brittle. It has so long been customary to use as many nails as could be conveniently driven, in fact, of fastening the shoe as if it were to a lifeless block of wood, that the fear is very commonly entertained that the shoe will not be held in its place with so few nails. Such fears are utterly groundless, as both theory and practice demonstrate. If the presence of a nail in the crust were a matter of no moment, and two or three more than are really necessary were merely useless, no great reason would exist for condemning the common practice of using too many nails, but it is far otherwise; the nails, aside from confining the natural expansion of the hoof, separate the fibres of the horn, which never, by any chance, become united again, but continue apart and unclosed, until, by degrees, they grow down with the rest of the hoof, and are finally, after repeated shoeing, removed by the knife.

As these holes cannot possibly grow down and be removed under three shoeings, it will be found, even with a small number of nails, that three times that number of holes must exist in the hoof all the while; and as they are often, from various causes, extended into each other, they necessarily keep it in a brittle, unhealthy state, and materially interfere with the future nail-hold. As the position of the hind foot, and the nature of its office, render it less liable to injury than the fore foot, consequently it less frequently lames; however, disease of the nervicular bone of this foot is by no means impossible. The same care should be taken as with the fore foot. Calks, although they may be turned down of perfectly even length on each side (which is seldom done), are objectionable appendages, and should be dispensed with, except, perhaps, for very heavy draughts, or when the roads are frozen or covered with ice.

TO PREVENT INTERFERING.

REMOVE the portion of crust that hits the ankle, and have the shoe set well under the foot.

The hoof should be lowest on the outside, to turn the ankle, that the other hoof may pass clear. The shoe should be light, and of narrow web, with only two nail holes on the inside, and those near the toe.

OVERREACHING.

YOUNG horses are more subject to overreaching than old ones. It very frequently disappears as the speed of the animal is increased. At a moderate gait, the front feet do not always get out of the way in time for the hind ones, as they are brought forward. Sometimes the heels are cut or bruised badly, and occasionally the shoes are torn from the front feet. To prevent this, have the front shoes a little lighter, the animal lifts them up more quickly. The hind shoes made a little heavier, causes him to lift them more slowly, and the difficulty is at once removed.

TO CURE CORNS.

CUT the horn well down, but not to the quick, fit the shoe so that it will not press upon the part, then saturate well with pine sap or gum, which is found exuding from pine trees when cut. Fill the part in nicely with tow, and put on the shoe, which must be so fitted as not to oblige the part to support, but very slightly, if any, the weight of the horse. Horses with corns must be oftener and more carefully shod than those free from them.

TO TELL A HORSE'S AGE.

THERE is only one sure way of telling the age of a horse, and that is by an examination of his teeth, and that only extends to a certain age, although an experienced horseman can guess very nearly for some time after that period. There are six teeth in the front part of a horse's mouth, above and below, called the gatherers, from which we may judge of his age. When a colt is foaled, he generally has no teeth in the front part of his mouth. In a few days, two come in the upper jaw, and two below; and again, after a few days, four more appear, but the corner teeth do not make their appearance until he is four or five months old; these twelve teeth remain unchanged in the front of the colt's mouth until he is about two years old, when he sheds the two centre nippers.

At three years old, a colt sheds the adjoining teeth. At four years old, the under or corner teeth. At five years old, the bridle tooth makes its appearance. At six years old, the cups leave the two centre teeth below. At seven years old, the cups leave the adjoining teeth. At eight years old, the cups leave the outer or corner teeth. At nine years old, the cups leave the two centre nippers, above. At ten years old, the cups leave the adjoining teeth. At eleven years old, the cups leave the corner upper teeth. At twelve years, or past, the groove in inside of the bridle tooth disappears in a horse. Mares very seldom have them.

TRICKS.

AS so many have expressed a desire to know how to teach their horses tricks, we have thought proper to explain how it can be done. Teaching a young horse a few tricks, makes him appear intelligent, and also serves to keep up an interest in him. It requires but two or three lessons a day, of half or three-quarters of an hour each, to accomplish anything you may desire.

TO TEACH A HORSE TO COME, AT THE CRACK OF THE WHIP.

ALL that is necessary to accomplish this, is to proceed precisely in the same manner as when giving the colt his first lesson. After having put on the war bridle, the cord should be three or four times as long;

then let him off the length of it, and if he does not come immediately after the crack of the whip and word, give him a little jerk. When he comes to you, always reward him by giving him sugar or apples. He will soon get so that you can at any time call him to you.

HOW TO TEACH A HORSE TO LAUGH.

PRICK him with a pin on the nose till he turns his lip up; then caress him well. He will soon learn that when you point towards him and say, "laugh," that it means a prick in the nose, if he does not turn his lip up.

TO SHAKE HANDS.

THIS is easily accomplished, by tying a short strap or piece of cord to the forward foot below the fetlock; then stand directly in front of the horse, and hold the end of the strap in your hand, and say, "shake hands, sir." After which pull immediately upon the strap, which will bring his foot forward, and which you are to accept as shaking hands; then, of course, you must caress and feed him, and keep him repeating, until when you make the demand he will bring the foot forward in anticipation of having it pulled up.

HOW TO MAKE A HORSE WALTZ.

TIE his head to his side, by means of a surcingle and cord, fastening the cord at the side, reaching from the mouth; touch him lightly with the whip. He has to go, and, of course, he must go around and around. He soon learns perfectly to waltz by the motion of the whip, the teacher still repeating the word "waltz."

HOW TO MAKE A TRICKY HORSE KISS YOU.

FIRST, teach him to bite at you by stinging him in the shoulder with a pin; thus when you go to sting him, to save himself he will put around his head. Have a piece of apple in your hand, put it up to your mouth, and he will soon learn that the words "kiss me" mean an apple for him in your mouth. This gives the horse the idea, so he will kiss you at command, by your making a slight backward motion of the head.

HOW TO MAKE A HORSE TO GO LAME.

TAP him on the fore leg till he holds it up, then caress him kindly; lead him with the left hand to the bit, and tap the left fore leg with a stick in your right hand;

repeat the word *lame*, *lame*, *lame*, and your horse will soon learn to hold up one leg at the command.

HOW TO MAKE A HORSE BOW.

PRICK him in the back with a pin, till he throws his head up and down the least bit; then take the pin away, and caress him kindly; repeat for a few times, until when you stand back and attract his attention he will nod his head, expecting a prick in the back.

HOW TO MAKE A HORSE SAY "NO."

PRICK him on the neck till he shakes his head, then remove the pin, caress him, repeat for a while, and your horse will soon shake his head when you raise your hand to your heart; be always sure to treat the animal kindly for well doing, and caress him when he deserves it, and he will repay you by his love for you and willingness to do your bidding.

HOW TO MAKE A HORSE WALK UP.

FIRST put a rope around his neck, bring it down through his mouth, back through the loop on the neck, jerk him till he raises his fore feet the least bit, then stop and caress him; then check him up tight to a surcingle—from the bit to the side ring is the better way; then jerk on the cord, and he will soon get up erect; repeat, still caressing him well for all he does; he will soon get up at the motion of the whip. You should, when practising him, repeat the words, "get up, sir!" It is in this manner I taught Tom Thumb to go up and down stairs, and to perform on the stage in different places, affording amusement to thousands of witnesses.

HOW TO MAKE A HORSE GET UP ON A BOX.

FIRST, raise the right foot to the box, hold it with your left hand, placing your right hand around the horse's left knee, pull hard; this throws the weight of the horse on his right leg, and he has got to come up; repeat a few times, and he will learn it perfectly.

TRAINING STEERS.

DRIVE your steer in a small yard, fenced so that he cannot escape. Then approach him gently, and if he runs, do not run after him, but follow slowly and quietly. Should he again run from you, do not strike him with the whip, or in any way frighten him, he will soon stand and permit you to approach him. Place then around his body a surcingle or strap, near the fore legs. Take a hame strap and buckle around the near fore foot; take a cord or rope, and pass it through under the surcingle, and tie to the strap which is around the foot. The cord should be twenty or thirty feet long, to permit him to run about you in the yard, without your pulling on it. Draw up on the rope to force him to move on three legs; approach him gently, till he will permit you to handle him as you please. Then hold up the near fore foot by the cord, with your left hand, and holding the whip in your right, pass it over his shoulder, and quietly touch him on the off side of his head, and at the same time, say, "haw!" continue thus till he moves his head towards you, for which caress him about the head and neck; repeat this till he will *haw* at the word, towards you. Should he attempt to run from you, pull on the strap, say, *haw*, at the same time touch him on the head with the whip. He will soon learn to stop at the word of command, in this way, and turn towards you readily. Then take off the rig and turn him loose. Then proceed with the mate in the same way, when you can turn it out, and by this time the other steer will be ready to receive another lesson. Drive it in the same yard, and repeat the lesson with a whip. Quietly touch on the near side of the head, and, at the same time, say, "gee!" until he will move around from you. Then caress him, till he will *gee* or *haw* readily. Go through the same lesson with the other. That is all you should try to do with them in four hours' time. Take both together in the yard; repeat this lesson till both understand what you desire of them. Take one of them near the wall; stand by his side; hit him gently on the head, at the same time say "back!" till he will step back; then caress him. Repeat, till he will go back readily at the word. Give each the same lesson. This manner of training steers will make them always do your bidding. When convenient, repeat the above lessons, with both together. Then put on the yoke, and let them go. One hour, at first, is long enough to become accustomed to the restraint of the yoke. Repeat this in the yard.

If the steers should ever run from you, which often occurs in an ordinary method of training, buckle a hame strap around the foot, bring it up through the surcingle back to the sled or wagon, between the steers. Let the man pull on the cord if they attempt to run away; this will pull up their feet; whip them over the head, which will stop them and break up the habit.

TO EDUCATE DOGS.

WE find dogs to be more easily educated than any other animal, and if kindly treated, is a willing and faithful servant to man; but if abused, will usually become cross and ugly. The dog, being naturally a companion to mankind, it becomes a duty to educate him, so that he will give credit to his trainer, and making him an agreeable and useful assistant to his owner. Judgment will be required to teach the dog to that which he is best adapted by nature: for instance, a Terrier will catch rats, and Setters naturally scent birds; be careful, therefore, in not urging upon them the performance of any tricks which are not in their nature to do.

TO EDUCATE THE SHEPHERD DOG TO DRIVE.

Commence with the dog at the age of three months, in some secluded place, hearing no words intended to guide him except his own name; he should know nothing of ordinary words in use towards dogs, and should not have been handled by persons. The first thing to teach him is to lead, placing a string around his neck, four or five feet long, in such manner as not to hurt him; stand still, and hold upon the cord till he ceases struggling to get away. One lesson should be given each day. The first lesson should be given to let him know he cannot get away, and in teaching him to come to you by pulling on the rope and saying, "*here*," using no other word that may confuse him. After he fully understands the meaning of the word "here," he will come to you when it is used; and as he comes to you, whether voluntarily or not, say "ho," and caress him. A lesson of thirty minutes, working him slowly and patiently, will be sufficient for each day.

Proceed with the lessons till he will come from any part of the yard at the word *here*. He has now learned that the word *ho* means you are through with him. You must now teach him the words *go* and *halt*. To do this, place yourself in a position opposite where he would desire to go: for instance, the opening of the enclosure you have chosen for these lessons; say "go," and by calling him, and urging him along. When he gets part of the way, say "halt," and at the same time pull upon the string, stopping him, and say "halt" again. Proceed thus till he has learned the meaning of the words. To teach the above four words it will take from one week to ten days, according to the sagacity of the animal.

TO TEACH HIM TO BARK AT THE WORD "SPEAK."

By holding up something which he wants very much—for instance, food, when he is quite hungry. If you wish him to go out, show him the door, and say, "go out;" the word "go" will start him, and, in a little while, he will become familiar with the word "out." Let him have a steady place to sleep, and teach him its name. If you already have a dog trained to drive, take him out with him to drive in the cattle. He will thus learn that they will run from him. Say nothing to him while he is with the other dog, unless he attempts to go to the *head* of the cattle. This you must not permit. After two or three times, take him out without the other dog, and allow him to run after the cattle, provided they are used to being driven by other dogs. It will not do to let him run where there is any danger of being turned upon. If he runs them too fast, say, "steady," and as you use words with him only when they mean something, he will be apt to pay attention, and go slower; if he does *not*, say, "halt," and then, "go," then "steady." He will gradually learn its meaning. Accustom him to the words "fetch" for sheep, and "get" for cattle. So, when you say *go* and *get* the the cattle, he knows you mean cattle instead of sheep or horse. Proceed to teach him the right from left, and to obey orders, in that respect, by the motion of your right hand, and the word "right." Then, by motion with the left hand, teach him the word "left." By these motions, and an appeal to the intelligence of the dog by your countenance and eyes, you can start him for the fields in any direction you choose, and he soon learns to do your bidding.

THE WATCH DOG.

For a good watch dog, select one of a breed adapted to the business, for any other will never be reliable. A barking dog, one that will be noisy at the approach of intruders, is the best.

To teach him, give him something to watch, saying, "take care of it," as you place him near the article. He will soon learn the word, and when being directed to any particular object, will faithfully guard it. While teaching him, allow no one but yourself to approach him without setting him on. You may have a stranger approach him, without setting him on, but urge him to drive the person away; and as soon as he starts, let the person run, you calling the dog back. While young, do not over-task him, but after having watched an article for some time, go up to him and say, "that will do," feeding him..

When you wish the dog to bite or go at any person or thing, you will teach him words the *reverse* of what you mean, such as "be still," "lie down," "get out," &c. So a person not understanding the words you have taught him the meaning of, will not be apt to get very near him, as they would naturally use these phrases, and be setting him on instead of quieting him as desired.

To call him yourself, use words not naturally used by others. These ideas are new and practical, and must meet with successful results, if used with skill.

THE TRICK DOG.

MANY amusing tricks may be taught to exhibit the wonderful sagacity of dogs. Perhaps a Spaniel dog is the most tractable of any, but a black-and-tan is quite as apt. A Scotch Terrier is also quick to learn.

TO TEACH HIM TO SIT UP.

Sit him up in the corner, and with a switch hit him lightly under the mouth, snapping your fingers, and say, "sit up." As he comes down, put him back, and repeat, till he will remain. Then say, "that will do," and call him down, and caress him; repeat this, till he will do it in any place as well as in the corner of a room. He will soon learn to do the trick at the word and snap of your fingers.

TO TEACH HIM TO SIT DOWN.

Press your hand upon his back toward his hind legs, and say, "sit down," at the same time tapping the floor with your foot. Tap him under the chin, to keep his head up. He will, after a few lessons, understand that tapping the floor means sit down.

TO STAND UP.

Take some food in your hand, and offer him, holding it well up, and say, "stand up." Repeat, till he will stand up readily, permitting him to rest his fore paws on your unoccupied hand, till he can stand easily alone. Then take him by the fore feet, lift him up quite hard, and say, "stand up." You can now combine this with the last two tricks, saying, *stand up, sit up, sit down, that will do.*

TO GET INTO A CHAIR.

Take your own way to coax him into the chair, using the word *chair* whenever you cause him to get into it. When he becomes familiar with the word, say, "go, and get into the chair." After he will do this, teach him to put his paws on the back, by saying, "put them up," or saying, "up!" assisting him at first. Then teach him to put his head down on his paws, by placing it there and repeating the word *down*, caressing him each time he complies. To have him hold his head up, tap him under the mouth, and say, "up," remembering to say "that will do," when you are through with the trick. You may teach him to jump over the chair, by playfully coaxing him to do so, saying, "jump."

TO MAKE HIM GO LAME.

Tap him with a little rod on the hind foot, saying, "lame;" then coax him along, and if he puts his foot down, hit him quite smartly on the foot, making him keep it up, till he will go lame at the word, and a motion of the rod. When you seat him in the chair, if he goes to jump down, stop him; teaching him to wait for the word *ho.* As he comes down with his fore feet on the floor, *steady* him by the word, and teach him to stop with his hind legs up in the chair; lead the way around as far as he can go, and then back again; if this is done on a stool, he can thus be taught to go all the way around, and is then ready to run on his forward legs. Do this as often as the chair trick is performed, saying "around;" after a while take him by the tail and lift him up, and switching his hind legs lightly, walk him around, saying, "around." He will soon learn to lift up his hind legs at the motion of the whip, and the words, "go around," and will perform a circle walking on his forward legs.

TO SIT ON A STOOL.

It is now easy to teach him to *sit down* on a low stool. You may then teach him to take a seat on the stool, by leading him around by his forward feet, and seating him on the stool, with his fore feet held up, saying, "seat."

TO TEACH HIM TO FIND THINGS.

Take something with which he is accustomed to play; call him up to you, and blindfold him, throw the article a short distance from you; if the dog has good scent, tell him you have *lost;* then remove the blindfold, and he will search and find it. Repeat this, throwing it farther each time, till you can throw anything you have held in your hand at a distance, you looking in the direction, saying, "I have *lost;*" he will search till he finds it. If the dog has *not* good scent, teach him to look down at the word *find*, and up at the word *up*.

By strictly observing these rules, which govern the teaching of dogs, you can teach them to climb ladders, fetch things to you, carry baskets, shut doors, roll over, and an innumerable number of tricks. But first of all, you must have perfect control of yourself. Never whip severely, and *never* get out of patience.

RULES AND REGULATIONS FOR THE GOVERNMENT OF TROTTING AND RACING, OVER THE UNION COURSE, LONG ISLAND.

1.—*Nature of Rules.*

ALL matches, or sweepstakes, which shall come off over the course will be governed by these rules, unless the contrary is mutually agreed upon by the parties making such match or stake.

2.—*Power of Postponement.*

In case of unfavorable weather, or unavoidable causes, all purses, matches, sweepstakes, announced to come off, to which the proprietors contribute, they shall have the power to postpone to a future day, upon giving notice of the same.

3.—*Qualifications of Horses Starting.*

Horses trained in the same stable, or owned in part by the same person within three days, shall not start for a purse; and horses so entered shall forfeit their entrance. A horse starting alone shall receive but one-half of the purse. Horses deemed by the judges not fair trotting horses, shall be ruled off previous to, or distanced at, the termination of the heat.

4.—*Entries.*

All entries shall be made under a seal, inclosing the entrance money (ten per cent. on the purse), and addressed to the proprietor, at such time and place as shall have been previously designated by advertisement.

5.—*Weight to be Carried.*

Every trotting horse starting for match, purse or stake, shall carry one hundred and forty-five pounds; if in harness, the weight of the sulky and harness not to be considered. Pacing horses subject to the same rule.

6.—*Distances.*

A distance for mile heats, best three in five, shall be one hundred yards; for one mile heats, eighty yards, and for every additional mile, an additional eighty yards.

7.—*Time between Heats.*

The time between heats shall be, for one mile, twenty minutes; for every additional mile, an additional five minutes.

8.—*Power of Judges.*

There shall be chosen by the proprietors of the course, or stewards, three judges to preside over a race for purses, and by them an additional judge shall be appointed for the distance stand; they may, also, during or previous to a race, appoint inspectors at any part of the course, whose reports, and theirs alone, shall be received of any foul riding or driving.

9.—*Difference of Opinion between Judges.*

Should a difference of opinion exist between the judges in the starting-stand on any question, a majority shall govern.

10.—*Judges' Duties.*

The judges shall order the horses saddled or harnessed five minutes previous to the time appointed for starting; any rider or driver causing undue detention after being called up, by making false starts or otherwise, the judges may give the word to start without reference to the situation of the horse so offending, unless convinced such delay is unavoidable on the part of the rider or driver; in which case not more than thirty minutes shall be consumed in attempting to start; and at the expiration of that time, the horse or horses ready to start shall receive the word.

11.—*Starting Horses.*

The pole shall be drawn for by the judges, the horse winning the heat shall, for the succeeding heats, be entitled to a choice of the track; on coming out on the last stretch, each horse shall retain the track first selected; any horse deviating shall be distanced.

12.—*Riders or Drivers.*

Riders or drivers shall not be permitted to start, unless dressed in jockey style.

13.—*Weight of Riders and Drivers.*

Riders and drivers shall weigh in the presence of one or more of the judges previous to starting; and, after a heat, are to come up to the starting stand, and not dismount until so ordered by the judges; any rider or driver disobeying, shall, on weighing, be precluded from the benefit of the weight of his saddle and whip, and if not full weight, shall be distanced.

14.—*Penalty for Foul Riding or Driving.*

A rider or driver, committing any act which the judges may deem foul riding or driving, shall be distanced.

15.—*Horses Breaking.*

Should any horse break from his trot or pace, it shall be the duty of the rider or driver to pull his horse to a trot or pace immediately; and, in case of the rider or driver refusing to do so, the penalty shall be that the next best horse shall have the heat. If the rider or driver should comply with the above, and he should gain by such break, twice the distanced so gained shall be taken away on the coming out; a horse breaking on the score shall not lose the heat by so doing.

16.—*The Winning Horse.*

A horse must win two heats to be entitled to the purse, unless he distanced all other horses in one heat. A distanced horse in a dead heat shall not start again.

17.—*Relative to Heats.*

A horse not winning one heat in three, shall not start for a fourth heat. When a dead heat is made between two horses, that if either had won the heat the race would have been decided, these two only shall start again. In races, best three in five, a horse shall win one heat in five to be allowed to start for the sixth heat, unless such horse shall have made a dead heat; such horses as are prevented from starting by this rule shall be considered drawn, and not distanced.

18.—*On Heats and Distances.*

If two horses each win a heat, and neither are distanced in the race, the one coming out ahead on the last heat to be considered the best. The same rule to be applied to horses, neither winning a heat and neither distanced. If one horse wins a heat, he is better than one that does not, provided he does not get distanced in the race; then the other, if not distanced, shall be the best. A horse that wins a heat, and is distanced, is better than one not winning a heat, and being distanced in the same heat. A horse distanced in the second heat is better than one distanced in the first heat.

19.—*Horses Drawn.*

Horses drawn before the conclusion of a race shall be considered distanced.

20.—*Outside Bets.*

In all matches made, play or pay; outside bets not to be considered play or pay, unless so understood by the parties.

21.—*Of Play or Pay Matches.*

All moneys bet play or pay matches by outside betters are not considered play or pay.

22.—*Betting; Absent Betters.*

A confirmed bet cannot be left off without mutual consent. If either party be absent at the time of trotting, and the money be not staked, the party present may declare the bet void in the presence of the judges, unless some party will stake the money bet for the absentee.

23.—*Compromised Matches.*

All bets made by outside betters on compromised matches are considered drawn.

24. *Betters of Odds, Etc.*

The person who bets the odds has the right to choose the horse or the field. When he has chosen his horse, the field is what starts against him; but there is no field unless one starts with him. If odds are bet without naming the horses before the trot is over, it must be determined as the odds were at the time of making it. Bets made in trotting are not determined till the purse is won, if the heat is not specified at the time of betting.

25.—*Horses Excluded from Starting, or Distanced.*

All bets made on horses precluded from starting (by rule 19), being distanced in the race, or on such horses against each other, shall be drawn.

26.—*In Cases of Dispute, and Improper Conduct.*

In all cases of dispute not provided for by the rules, the judges for the day will decide finally. In case of a trot or match being proved to their satisfaction to have been made or conducted improperly or dishonestly on the part of the principals, they shall have the power to declare all bets void.

27.—*The Size of Whips to be Used.*

No rider or driver shall be allowed any other than a reasonable length of whip, namely: for saddle horses, two feet ten inches; sulky, four feet eight inches; wagon, five feet ten inches.

28.—*In Case of Accidents.*

In case of accidents but five minutes shall be allowed over the time specified in rule No. 10, unless the judges think more time necessary.

29.—*Judges' Stand.*

No person shall be allowed in the judges' stand but the judges, reporters, and members, at the time of trotting.

30.—*In Case of Death.*

All engagements are void upon the decease of either party being determined.

RECIPES.

THE following recipes have been gathered from sources entitled to the fullest confidence, as remedies of value to all owners of horses, and are presented with the hope of doing good.

A CURE FOR HEAVES, NEVER BEFORE PUBLISHED.

Take a common stone jar, fill it with eggs, cover them with cider vinegar, and let it stand till the vinegar eats up the shells. Then stir all together. Take a lump of lime about the size of a goose egg, slack it in hot water, using about one quart of water. Add one-half pint of the lime water to a quart of the egg mixture. Give a teacupful, at feeding time, in feed, three times a day.

A REMEDY TO CURE THE HEAVES.

One-half pint of turpentine, 2 oz. assafœtida, 2 oz. aloes, 4 oz. lobelia seed, 1 quart of whisky, 2 oz. of sal ammoniac, 4 oz. salæratus, 1 oz. of camphor.

Dose, one tablespoonful once a day.

TO CURE WORMS IN HORSES.

One drachm white hellebore in powder, 1 drachm sulphate of iron in powder, 1 oz. flaxseed meal.

The above for one dose, mixed with bran mash, given at night. Repeat in forty-eight hours, if the horse is old. Two doses are enough for the worst case.

TO CURE THE SCRATCHES
in the shortest time ever known.

USE two tablespoonfuls of lard, and one tablespoonful of slacked lime; brush out the dirt and dust from the foot; *use no water.* Apply the salve, well mixed, twice each day. It will cure the worst cases in **4 to 6 days.**

Another remedy:

Hydrate of potassa, 10 grains; pulverized nutgalls, ½ oz.; white lead, pulverized opium, each ¼ oz.; lard, ¼ lb. Wash with soap-suds, rub dry, and apply the mixture night and morning. Give purging ball.

COLIC OR GRIPES.

Symptoms:—Pawing, manifesting a desire to lie down, and, without doing so, commence pawing again. As the symptoms increase, the animal cannot be kept on his feet; he frequently falls as if shot; pulse not altered from natural condition. Intervals of rest, together with the condition of the pulse, distinguish the disease from inflammation of the bowels.

Treat as follows:

Frequent injections of soap and water, and give internally, spirits of nitre, 1 oz.; laudanum, 1 oz.; water, ½ pint; mix for drench. This may be repeated in twenty minutes, if relief is not obtained.

Another remedy, giving *instant* relief:

From 5 to 10 drops of chloroform, given on sugar, I have never known to fail giving immediate relief. I have known men to be from home, and have their horses taken with this disease, and use this remedy, and in thirty minutes the horses were able to be driven.

FOR INFLAMMATION OF THE LUNGS.

First, bleed thoroughly; then give tinc. veratrum, ½ oz.; laudanum, 4 oz.; tincture aconite, ½ oz.; shake well, and give a teaspoonful every three hours, in a pint of water, well sweetened, and, if the pulse is not reduced in a short time, increase the dose to a tablespoonful, until the fever abates. As soon as the horse recovers so as to eat and lie down naturally, keep him on hay, with a few carrots or potatoes, and daily give a bran mash, with saltpetre, pulverized antimony and sulphur, for a week or ten days, and you will prevent dropsy of the chest, which usually follows this disease.

SPAVIN.

This being a valuable recipe, it is worth money to any man dealing in horses.

Euphorbium, 5 oz.; cantharides, fine, 2 oz.; iodine, 1 oz., dissolved in alcohol; red precipitate, ½ oz.; corrosive sublimate, 1 oz.; quicksilver, ½ oz.; hog's lard, 6 oz.; white turpentine, 6 oz.; verdigris, ¼ lb. Melt the lard and turpentine together, then, while hot, add the others, except the quicksilver, which must be stirred in as it becomes cold. Mix well. When cold, it is fit for use. Rub it in well on the spavin every day for three days, then wash clean with soap-suds, and omit for three days; then repeat for three days, and so continue until a perfect cure is effected. Should it blister, use more cautiously.

BONE SPAVIN.

One-half pound of blood root; 1 quart of alcohol; 2 oz. tannin; ¼ lb. alum. Mix and let stand. Shaking several times a day till the strength is all in the alcohol, and bathe the spavin twice a day, rubbing with the hand.

FOR WINDGALLS.

Olive oil, 2 oz.; nitric acid, ¼ oz. Rub as much in every day, or every second or third day, as will bear without starting the hair.

FOR INFLAMED SWELLINGS OR LAMED SHOULDERS.

Equal parts oil amber, oil spike, gum camphor, and ether. Should be shaken well before using, and well rubbed in with the hand.

HIDE BOUND.

This condition of the skin is usually produced by any derangement of system. Medicine of an alterative character is here indicated. The most successful remedy is sulphur, pulverized, 8 oz.; nitrate of potassa, pulverized, 3 oz.; black antimony, pulverized, 2 oz.; sulphate of iron, 4 oz. Mix well together, and give one tablespoonful twice a day.

Another good remedy:

Take saltpetre, 4 oz.; crude antimony, 1 oz.; sulphur, 2 oz. The saltpetre and antimony should be finely pulverized, then add the sulphur, and mix well together. Dose: tablespoonful of the mixture in bran mash daily.

HOW TO DISTINGUISH BETWEEN DISTEMPER AND GLANDERS.

The discharge from the nose in Glanders will sink in water. In Distemper it will not.

DISTEMPER.

All catarrhal affections are classed by horse owners under the head of distemper. Common catarrh, epidemic catarrh, laryngitis, bronchitis, and all other diseases, accompanied by nasal discharges, are regarded by horsemen as one and the same.

The following remedy is to cure distemper in its simple form, as we find it in colts soon after the disease commences. If there is swelling under the jaws, poultice the throat with flaxseed meal, or bread and milk. Apply mustard and vinegar, and give internally one of the following powders in feed: pulverized gentian, 2 ounces; sulph. copper, 1 oz.; pulverized ginger, 6 drachms; mix, and divide into 8 powders.

INFLUENZA.

For several years past a disease has been more or less prevalent in various sections of this country, known to the Veterinary as epidemic catarrh or influenza. The symptoms of this disease are so various in different animals—no two being precisely alike—that a variety of opinions are current concerning it and its nature; and, as a consequence, various other diseases are often confounded with it. The usual or leading symptoms are a slight watery or mucous discharge from the nose; eyelids presenting a reddish appearance; matter collects in the corner of the eyes; pulse feeble; great debility, as shown by the quick, feeble action of the heart--a symptom rarely absent; membrane of nose much reddened; sore throat and cough; occasionally the feet become fevered as in founder, causing much stiffness, and might be easily taken for that disease.

Treatment:—This being a typhoid disease, it requires a sustaining treatment, or success will be very doubtful. In the early stage of this disease, give the first two days ten drops of tincture of aconite, or bryonia, in a little water, every six hours; after which give a pail of water to drink, and, once a day, 1 oz. spirits of nitre, or 2 drachms extract of belladonna; and give in the feed, three times a day, one of the following powders: gentian root, saltpetre, and anise seed, of each 1 oz.; sulphate of quinine, 1 drachm; mix, and divide into eight powders. The throat should be bathed with mustard and vinegar; or with linseed oil, 3 oz., spirits of hartshorn, 1 oz. Mix together. No hay or corn should be given, but scalded oats or wheat bran, with linseed tea, or oatmeal gruel, should constitute the diet. I would recommend a few carrots. But above all, good nursing is to be desired, and by strictly following the foregoing instructions a successful result is probable.

GLANDERS.

This is one of the most fatal diseases to which the horse is subject. It is propagated in most cases by contagion, the infection being disseminated by seed from the nasal discharge, not, as many suppose, by the breath. According to eminent foreign authors, the disease has its origin also in a vitiated state of the blood, and this may result from improper treatment or neglect of almost any disease to which he is liable. In its early stage it appears to be only a slight inflammation of the inner membrane of the nose, not, however, attended with the usual florid red characterising inflammation, but of a paler hue, and afterwards becoming darker. The first marked symptom is a discharge from the nose, scarcely to be distinguished at first from the natural moisture, either by its color or consistence, and generally coming from one nostril only, and that the left one. In appearance it is thin and transparent, closely resembling the natural discharge, a little increased in quantity, and sometimes continues in this doubtful stage for several weeks or months. Instances are indeed known where it has existed for several years before it became fully developed. In such cases it is attended with no loss of appetite, no cough, or apparent illness of any kind, with little enlargement of the glands under the jaw, and at the same time the horse is capable of communicating disease.

Too many of these horses, with a decided glanderous discharge from the nose and adherent glands under the jaw, are found on our roads, or are employed in agriculture, which (although they are otherwise in good health, and perform their work well) should not be permitted; for by such means the contagion is widely spread. No cough accompanies real glanders in any of its stages, except the last, which is usually soon cut short by death.

In addition to the preceding tokens foı discovering at an early period the true glanders from other disorders, let the nostrils be closely examined. In the real glanders, the left or running nostril will be found of a deeper color than ordinary, while the other, or dry nostril, is of a paler color, or almost white.

The reader must bear in mind the varied color of the nostril in deciding all cases of this character. Also that in colds, &c., both nostrils run.

Before the disease finishes its course, both sides of the nose and head become affected—the ulcers extend down the windpipe, and fasten upon the lungs. The virus, secreted by and discharged from the ulcers, is absorbed and carried through the whole system, and soon puts an end to the creature's miserable existence. The best preventives of glanders are dry, clean, well-ventilated stables, moderate exercise, green food, when it can be procured, and roots in the winter.

The disease may be cured in its early stages, or before ulcers are formed in the nose, or the lumps under the jaw adhere to the bone, by turning the animal on a dry pasture, by proper attention to the bowels, and by use of alterative medicines, to work the poisons out of the system. Should the bowels require loosening, give the common purge. For purifying the blood, the condition powder is the most effectual remedy. The owner must beware of putting the horse to hard labor too soon, after having been turned out as before directed, as the disease is liable to return on subsequent confinement, even after the running at the nose has entirely disappeared. It is conceded by all that, when this disease is once seated, it cannot be cured; and humanity dictates, and economy should prompt us to terminate the animal's existence at once. This course has now become an imperative duty, as the fact is established that man is susceptible to the contagion; and there are numerous cases on record where those who have had the care of glandered horses have fallen victims to this disease.

CHRONIC COUGH.

This is generally the consequence of neglected catarrhal affections, worms, &c. For treatment, give twice each day Barbadoes aloes, 2 oz.; pulv. foxglove (or digitalis), 1 oz.; linseed meal, 13 oz. Mix with molasses. Dose, 1 oz.

Another remedy is, sal ammoniac, 1 oz.; squills, pulv., ½ oz.; aloes, pulv., 1 oz.; linseed meal, 16 oz.; mix with molasses, and divide into four balls; to be given one each night for four days.

TREATMENT FOR RHEUMATISM.

Poultice the feet with mustard and flaxseed meal. Give internally of nux vomica, 1 oz.; pulv. gentian root, 1½ oz.; pulverized ginger, 1 oz. Mix, and divide into 12 powders; give one every night in the feed, keep the body warm, and give no corn.

LOCK-JAW.

This disease generally arises from nail wounds in the feet, or from sharp metallic substances taken into and wounding the stomach or intestines. The first symptoms of the disease are observed about the ninth or tenth day after the injury is done, which are a straggling or stiffness of the hind legs, to which succeed in a few days the following: on elevating the head, a spasmodic motion of the membrane in the inner corner of the eye will be observed, showing little more than the white of the eye; the muscles of the jaws become rigid; the tongue is swollen, and the mouth is filled with saliva; the ears are erect, the nose poked out; the nostrils expand; respiration becomes disturbed; and, finally, the jaws become firmly set, and the bowels constipated.

Treatment:—Tinct. of aconite, 2 drs.; tinct. of belladonna, 2 drs.; water, ½ oz. Mix, and give 40 drops every 4 hours on the tongue; keep a ball of aloes in the mouth for several days. There is no fear of giving too much. I have known half a pound to be given in a few days with good success. Hydrocyandic acid, 20 drops in a little water, and put upon the tongue every four hours, is an excellent remedy. Foment the jaws with bags of hops steeped in hot water, and bathe the line of the back from the pole to the croup with mustard and vinegar. Be careful not to allow the animal to be unnecessarily excited by noises and confusion about him. Go about him quietly; keep a pail of bran slop before him all the time. If the foot has been injured, poultice with flaxseed meal, and keep the wound open until a healthy action has been established.

FOUNDER REMEDY.

Give from 1 to 4 ounces of saltpetre, according to the severity of the case. For a severe case, draw about one gallon of blood from the neck; then dre... with linseed oil, 1 quart; rub the fore legs with water as hot as can be borne without scalding, continuing the washing till the horse is perfectly limber.

HORSE OINTMENT.

Resin, 4 oz.; beeswax, 4 oz.; honey, 2 oz.; lard, 8 oz.; melt these articles slowly, bringing gradually to a boil; remove from the fire, and slowly add a little less than a pint of spirits of turpentine, stirring all the time this is being added, and stir till cool. This is an extraordinary ointment for bruises of the flesh, or hoof, or broken knees, galls or bites, or when a horse is gelded to heal and keep off flies.

CONDITION POWDER.

Fœnugrec, cream of tartar, gentian, sulphur, saltpetre, resin, black antimony, and ginger, of each 1 oz.; cayenne, ½ oz.; all finely pulverized. Mix thoroughly. It is used for yellow water, hide bound, colds, coughs, distemper, and all other diseases where a condition powder is needed. They carry off gross humors, and purify the blood.

Dose:—In ordinary cases one tablespoonful once a day. In extreme cases give twice daily. This powder has never failed to give entire satisfaction.

MAGIC LINIMENT.

Take 2 oz. oil of spike; 2 oz. origanum; 2 oz. hemlock; 2 oz. wormwood; 4 ounces sweet oil; 2 oz. spirits ammonia; 2 ounces gum camphor; 2 oz. spirits turpentine; 1 quart proof spirits. Mix well and bottle for use. Cork tight. For sprains, bruises, or lameness of any kind, this liniment is unsurpassed. This is the same liniment, leaving out the turpentine, which has achieved such wonderful cures for human ailment.

A more simple liniment can be made by putting into spirits of turpentine all the gum camphor it will cut. For ordinary purposes it is fit for use; but if you wish to reduce pain, add as much laudanum as there is turpentine.

FRENCH PASTE FOR BONE SPAVIN.

Corrosive sublimate, quicksilver, and iodine, of each 1 oz., with sufficient lard to form a paste. Rub the quicksilver and iodine together, and add the sublimate, and finally add the lard, rubbing thoroughly. Shave off the hair the size of the bone enlargement, then grease all around it, but not where the bone is shaved off. This prevents the action of the medicine only upon the spavin; rub in as much of the paste as will lie on a five cent piece, each morning for four mornings only, and in from six to eight days the spavin will come out; then wash out the wound with suds, soaking well for an hour or two, which removes the poisonous effects of the medicine, and facilitates the healing, which can be done by any healing salve. I prefer the horse ointment to any other.

LINIMENT FOR SPAVIN, SPLINT CURBS, ETC.

Oils of spike, origanum, cedar, British, and spirits of turpentine, of each 1 oz.; pulverized Spanish flies, ½ oz. Apply once in six or nine days.

RING-BONE REMEDY.

Pulverized cantharides, oils of spike, origanum, amber, cedar, British, and Barbadoes tar, of each 2 oz.; oil of wormwood, 1 oz.; spirits of turpentine, 4 oz.; lard, 3 lbs. Melt the lard slowly, and add the other ingredients, stirring well till cool; clip off the hair, and apply by rubbing in and heating. In about three days, or when done running, wash off with suds and apply again. In recent cases, two or three applications will cure; old cases require more time.

POLL-EVIL AND FISTULA.

Common potash, ¼ oz.; extract of belladonna, 12 drachms; gum Arabic, ¼ oz. Dissolve the gum in as little water as possible; then, having pulverized the potash, unless it is moist, mix the gum water with it, and it will soon dissolve; add the belladonna; mix, and it is ready to use.

The best method for getting this into the pipes, is by means of a small syringe, after having cleansed the sore well with suds. Repeat once in two days, until the callous pipes, and hard, fibrous base around the poll-evil or fistula are completely destroyed.

TO SCATTER POLL-EVIL.

Take a quantity of mandrake root, bruise and boil it, strain and boil down until rather thick; then form an ointment, simmering with sufficient lard for the purpose. Anoint the swelling once a day until cured. It has cured them after they were broken out, by putting it in the pipes a few times; also, anointing around the sore.

ANTISPASMODIC TINCTURE,
For Man or Beast.

Oils of cajuput, cloves, peppermint, annise, of each 1 oz.; of alcohol, 1 quart. Mix together, and bottle for use. Dose, for horse, 1 oz. every 15 minutes, in a little whisky and warm water, sweetened with molasses. Continue till relieved.

Dose for man, one teaspoonful.

PHYSIC BALL.

Barbadoes aloes, 1 lb.; syrup buckthorn, 3 oz.; cod-liver oil, 3 oz. Melt the whole, and stir till cool. In winter, add a little water, make into 18 pills, and give 1 every four hours, or as much as will move the bowels.

DIURETIC DROPS.

These drops are reliable in cases of stoppage of water, foul water, or inflammation of the kidneys. Take sweet spirits of nitre,

4 oz.; balsam copaiba, 2 oz.; oil of juniper, 2 oz.; spirits of turpentine, 2 oz.; gum camphor, pulv., 1 oz. Mix all together, and shake well; bottle, and it is fit for use, for man or beast, under all circumstances where a diuretic is required.

Dose for horse, 1 oz. in half a pint of milk, once in six hours.

Dose for man, 1 teaspoonful, in a tablespoonful of milk, once in six hours.

Be sure to shake the mixture up well before pouring out for use.

AN OINTMENT FOR ALL BRUISES, SCRATCHES, HEEL GREASE, SADDLE GALLS, ETC.

Take 3 oz. white lead, 3 oz. of lard, 1 oz. burnt alum, and 5 grains calomel. If the sore is of long standing, use 10 grains of calomel.

SWEENY LINIMENT.

Alcohol, and spirits of turpentine, of each 8 oz.; camphor gum, pulverized cantharides and tincture of capsicum, of each 1 oz.; oil of spike 3 oz. Bathe this liniment in with a hot iron, and faithfully follow till a cure is effected.

NERVE AND BONE LINIMENT.

Take beef's gall, 1 quart; alcohol, 1 pint; volatile liniment, 12 oz.; spirits of turpentine, 1 lb.; oil of origanum, 4 oz.; aqua ammonia, ½ pint; oil of amber, 3 oz.; tincture of catharides, 6 oz. Mix.

ENGLISH STABLE LINIMENT.

Oil of spikes, aqua ammonia, and oil of turpentine, of each 2 oz.; sweet oil, and oil of amber, of each ½ oz.; oil of origanum, 1 oz. Mix.

HOOF LINIMENT, FOR CONTRACTED HOOF.

Venice turpentine, ½ pint; aqua ammonia, 2 oz.; salts of nitre, 1 oz.; benzine, 1 oz.;

alcohol, 3 oz. Apply to the edge of the hair and to the hoof, twice a day for the first three days; once a day for the next three days; after that, once in two, three, or four days, as the case may require.

REMEDY FOR BOTTS.

Take oil of turpentine, 8 oz.; alcohol, 1 quart. Mix and bottle for use. Dose, 4 to 5 oz. in the horse's feed, once a day for 8 days, will effectually remove every vestige of botts.

TO PREVENT HORSES BEING TEASED BY FLIES.

Take ½ lb. of walnut or butternut leaves, and pour upon them 3 quarts of cold water; let it infuse one night, and pour the whole next morning into a kettle, and let it boil for a quarter of an hour. When cold it is fit for use.

No more is required than to moisten a sponge, and before the horse goes out of the stable, let those parts most likely to be irritated be well smeared over with the liquor, between and upon the ears, neck, flanks, &c.

TREATMENT OF WOUNDS.

Wounds are caused by accidents of various kinds, when the skin is much torn from the flesh. If you are at hand while the wound is quite fresh, take a square-pointed needle, and a waxed thread, and sew it up. Be sure to put the needle in straight, one side over against the other, draw the skin tight, tie a knot, and cut off the thread; then take another stich about an inch off, till it is all nicely drawn together. It is quite wrong to sew up a wound as you would a piece of cloth; the thread should be cut after each stitch. When you do not see the wound till the place is growing dead, and the skin is drawing up, then take off the loose skin; for if you permit it to remain, it will leave a blemish.

WASH FOR FOUL ULCERS.

Permanganate of Potassa, 1 drachm; pure water, 6 fluid ounces. Clean the sore once or twice a day, with a quart of water, to which a large tablespoonful of the wash has been added, using a soft sponge.

The discoloration of the solution indicates its complete loss of power as a disinfectant.

The bottle must be kept tightly corked, as impurities in the air will, in time, impair its value.

HEALING SALVE FOR ABRASIONS AND CUTS.

Oxide of zinc, 4 drachms; fresh lard, 1 oz.; carbolic acid, 6 grains. Melt the lard, and stir in the oxide of zinc, which must be very finely powdered; add the carbolic acid and mix thoroughly. Apply twice a day to the wound. This salve is very valuable for its healing properties, and will be found of special service, if there is any foul discharge.

HOW TO CLEAN AND OIL HARNESS.

First take the harness apart, having each strap and piece by itself; then wash it with warm water and Castile soap. When cleansed, black each part with the following dye: 1 oz. extract of logwood; 12 grains bichrómate of potash—both pounded fine; put into two quarts of boiling rain-water, and stir till all is dissolved. When cool, it may be used. It may be bottled and kept for future use, if desired. It may be applied with a shoe brush. When the dye has struck in, you may oil each part with neatsfoot oil, applied with a paint brush. For second oiling, use one-third castor oil and two-thirds neatsfoot oil, mixed. A few hours after, wipe clean with a woolen cloth, which gives the harness a glossy appearance. This preparation does not injure the leather or stitching, but makes it soft and pliable, and obviates the necessity of oiling as often as is necessary by the ordinary method. When the harness is removed from the horse, take a woolen cloth or cha mois skin, kept for the purpose, and wipe off the dust and all moisture from rain or perspiration, and when the harness is nearly dry, rub the damper parts very thoroughly with a second cloth or skin, until they are quite soft and pliable.

The bits, and plated mountings, should be cleaned and rubbed with a slightly oiled rag, before the harness is finally hung in its place; the harness should be protected from dust either by a covering of cloth, or by hanging in a closet. Whenever the leather becomes dry and hard, it should be cleaned and oiled according to the foregoing directions.

AN EXPOSITION

OF THE

DUNBAR SYSTEM OF HORSE SHOEING,

AND TREATMENT OF THE HORSE'S FOOT,

As taught to the Farriers of the United States Army by ALEXANDER DUNBAR, *under the authority of the Joint Resolution of Congress, and for which Dunbar received twenty-five thousand dollars. Highly recommended to the U. S. Army by Robert Bonner and George Wilkes.*

INSTRUCTIONS FOR FITTING AND DRIVING THE SHOE.

The first thing to be done is to carefully examine the horse's feet all around, to see that they are of a natural shape, taking care to abstain from any action that will tend to excite the horse.

The shoes should be removed one at a time, and the nails carefully drawn after the clinches are cut, one at a time; anything like tearing off the shoe by main force should by all means be avoided.

The shoe being removed, the rasp should then be used on the edge of the foot where the shoe has been, removing all dirt and gravel which may have accumulated there, and thus prevent injury to the shoeing knife.

If the foot is healthy and of a natural shape, and has been shod regularly, no alteration is required, but simply to pare out the sole of the foot, removing the bors entirely, and opening out the heels back. The surface of the frog should be trimmed off a very little, but the sides should never be cut.

By reference to Plate No. 12 the exact idea of the system of paring the foot may be gained. It has been practiced successfully, and is recommended for the simple reason that by the system of removing the bors and opening out the heels, contraction is prevented, and the frog retains its natural shape, because all pressure is removed from each side.

The foot should not be scooped out so as to leave the wall projecting without any support; for the wall of the hoof is the base upon which the horse travels, and this should be supported by a sufficiency of the sole as a "ground surface." The shoes should be removed and the feet prepâred one at a time.

In fitting a shoe to the foot, after it has been thoroughly prepared, the farrier should take hold of the foot and see that the shoe is perfectly easy on the heels, and that he has sufficient room all around in the manner illustrated on Plate No. **11.** If the shoe is found to fit well everywhere, he will take the foot between his knees, and placing the shoe properly, drive the nails with great care, so that the shoe cannot get out of its proper place. When the nails are started he should hammer them home lightly, or according to the foot he is working on. The three nails on the inside and outside, toward the toe, should always be driven a little tighter than the heel nails, so as to prevent pressure on the heels. No man should be in a hurry in shoeing a horse, but should always be careful in fitting and driving the shoe as instructed.

A shoe should never be fitted tightly, unless the coffin-bone has too much play; then it should be fitted tight around the toe and each quarter, as far as the nail-holes extend back, in order to contract the foot, and bring the coffin-bone to its proper place. Such cases are, however, very rare.

The heels of the shoe should never be allowed to curve inward toward the frog, and the foot should be prepared so as to prevent any pressure from the shoe on the heel, in the manner shown by Plate No. 14, at the same time allowing the bearing of the shoe to be perfectly equal.

If the horse has a long foot it should be shortened on the toe as much as possible—the more the better—for the hoof grows out more quickly at the toe; and it is necessary, because in a case of this kind the coffin-bone is necessarily out of its proper position, and the operation of shortening the toe must be continued until it resumes its natural shape; but a close operation, and working the horse at the same time, is not recommended, because the foot can be brought to its proper shape by cutting gradually in time.

After the cutting has been performed, a shoe should be fitted so as to have the pressure on each quarter, and with heels, if the horse's heels are naturally low, in order to prevent a sudden change.

A horse should be reshod at least once a month.

Plate No. 3—*Paring out the Foot.*—By reference to this plate it will be seen what a difference there exists between the system recommended and practiced by Mr. Dunbar, and the old style practiced and recommended by all authorities on the subject heretofore.

The bors should be *cut away entirely*, removing the pressure from the frog, and cutting out the heel. By this system of paring the foot a ground surface will always be left, commencing at the heel and expanding gradually, as illustrated by the plates "A" to "C;" the sides of the frog should never be cut, but the top should be cut down sufficiently to allow it to be clear of the ground after the shoe is fitted. The cleft of the frog should always be cleaned out thoroughly every time the shoe is renewed.

Plates Nos. 4 and 5—*Long Feet before and after Cutting.*—A horse with a long foot, as will be easily seen, will suffer from an undue pressure on the heels (see article on Corns), causing corns, and in addition to that, if the foot is not shortened in time, it will cause the coffin-bone to lose its proper shape, but this can be remedied by shortening the toe every time the horse is shod, thus keeping the foot in its proper shape.

The common practice of fitting a shoe tight on the heels, to prevent interfering, is entirely wrong; an interfering horse does not strike with his heel, but with the inner side of the toe, not further back than the heel-nails, both hind and forward. To prevent this, the shoe should be fitted wider on the *inner* than on the *outer* heel. A horse that interferes should be carefully examined by the farrier before shoeing, who

No. 3.

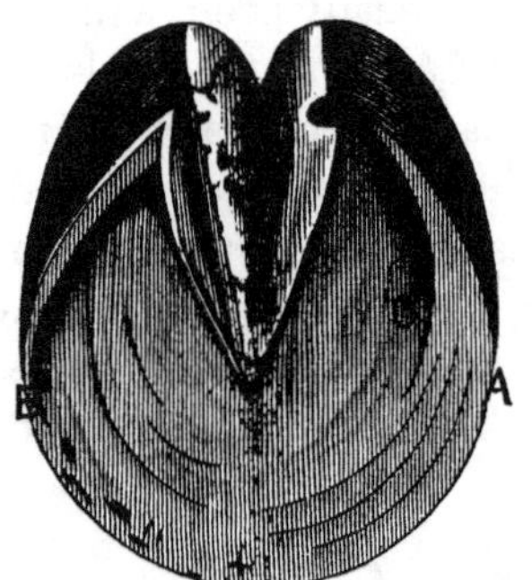

a New style. *b* Old style.

PARING THE FOOT.

No. 4.

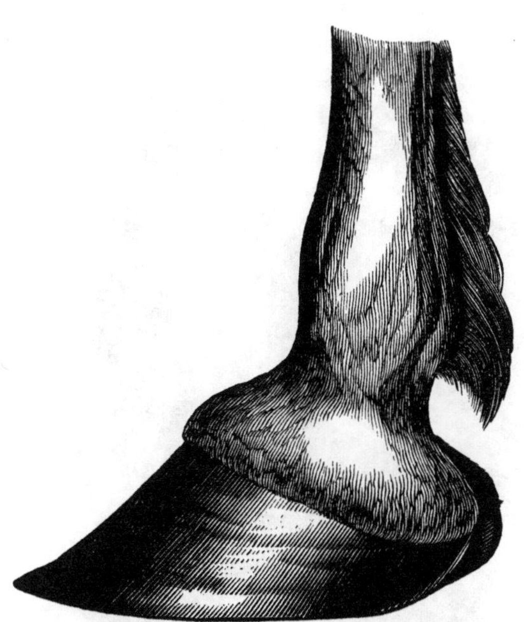

Long Foot—Before Treatment.

No. 5.

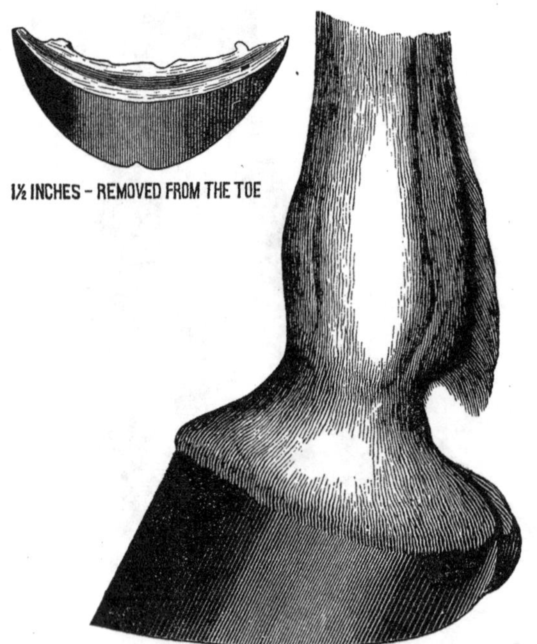

LONG FOOT—AFTER TREATMENT.

No. 10.

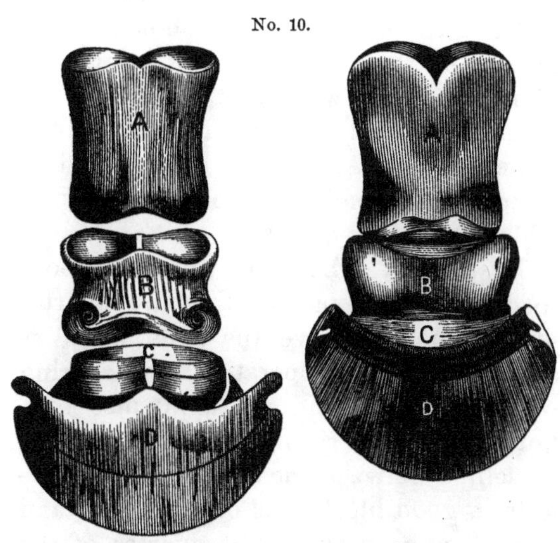

FIG. 1.
a Upper pastern.
b Lower pastern.
c Navicular bone.
d Coffin-bone.

FIG. 2.
a Upper pastern.
b Lower pastern.
c Navicular bone.
d Coffin-bone, with the horny laminæ.

COFFIN-BONE.

will notice particularly the shape of his feet. If the animal stands *inward* and interferes, the *outside* quarter should be cut down, and thus throw the foot level; and if he stands outward and interferes, the *inside* quarter should be cut down for the same reason. After this a shoe should be fitted with no nails on the inner quarter, which should be *thickest.*

To prevent a horse travelling pigeon-toed is simply to pare off the inner quarter of the toe, and have the shoe fitted as above. By this operation the bearing will be level. This will apply also to a horse for light riding, and for a horse travelling between the shafts; but for the latter a good block heel on the outer, and a small one on the inner quarter of the shoe should be made; the toe also to be made thick in proportion, to make the bearing level.

Plate No. 10 is a representation of a perfectly healthy coffin-bone, with the upper and lower pastern and navicular bones

No. 11.

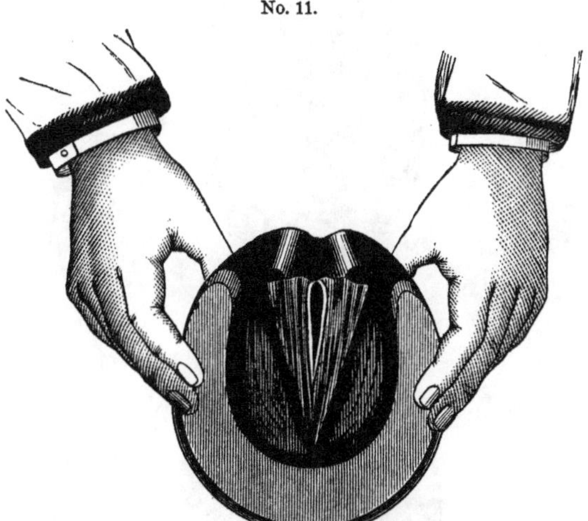

FITTING A SHOE TO REMOVE PRESSURE FROM THE HEEL.

No. 12.

Contracted.

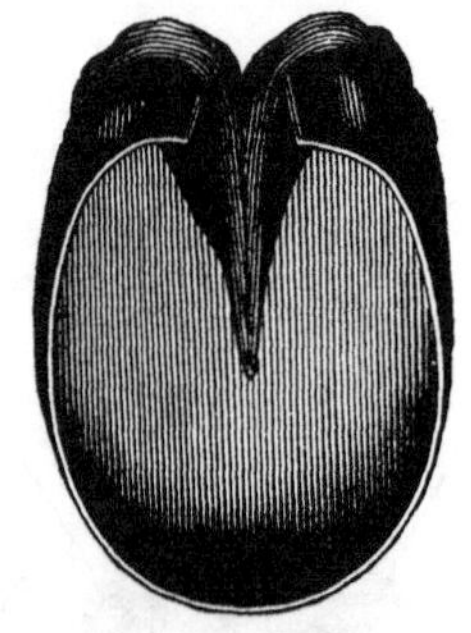

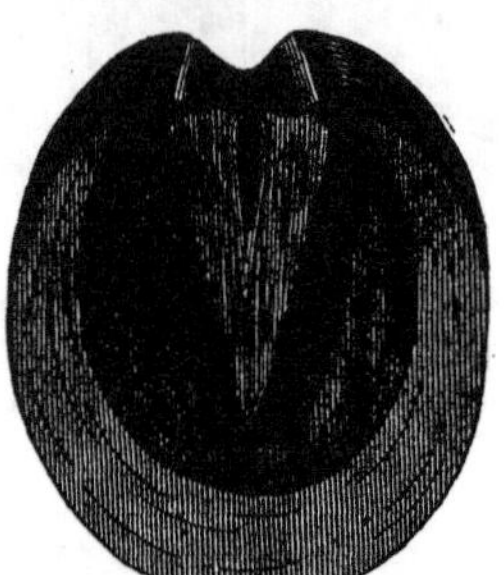

Natural.

No. 13.
Old style paring out the foot.

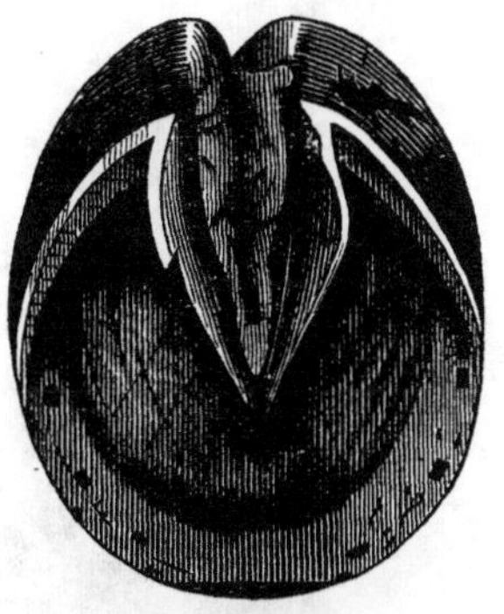

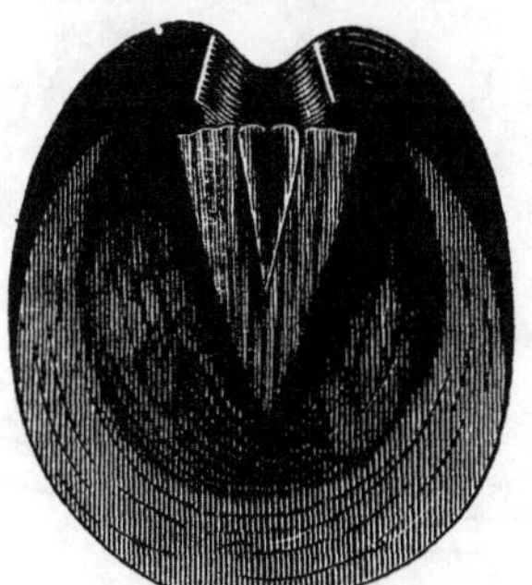

New style.

No. 14.

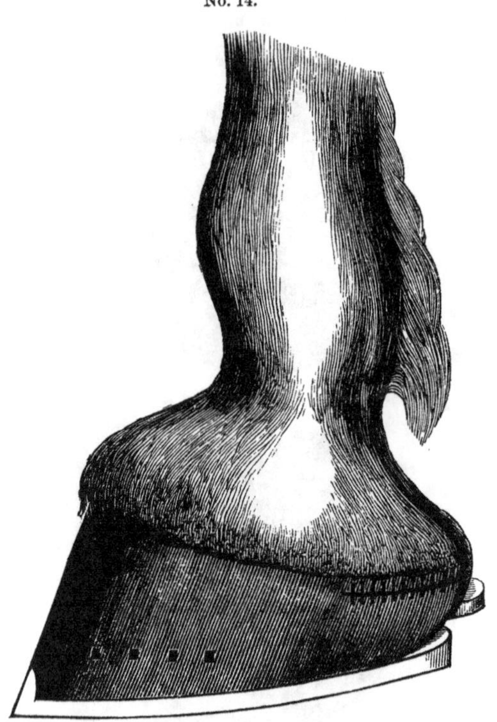

CONTRACTED FOOT AFTER TREATMENT.

front, and reverse sides. The system recommended by the author is intended to prevent any pressure whatever on the wings of the coffin-bone. Anything that prevents the perfectly free action of the coffin-bone will cause "navicular disease," and "ossified cartilages." After a foot is pared, as recommended in this, so as to be easily expanded, the wings of the coffin-bone, which are the widest part, should be protected by a wide shoe, and there should be no pressure whatever on the heels.

CORNS.

The pressure of the bor on one side of the seat of the disease, and of the horny substance of a contracted heel on the other side, added to a tight shoe, causes inflammation, which, when it becomes chronic, is styled a *corn.*

A corn may be detected by paring the foot close. It is not necessary, as recommended by some authorities, to use a pair of pincers, squeezing the hoof all around to find the corn, thereby giving the horse unnecessary pain. They are to be found only in the heel, and do not result from bruises, but from pressure.

Treatment.—The shoe having been removed, the inside of the hoof should be pared out thoroughly all around, and if a long hoof it should be shortened. If the corn is visible, the heel should be pared down and the bors weakened, opening the heel as far back as possible (see Plate No. 11), and fitting an open shoe, so as to throw the pressure off the heel. The pressure having been removed, the corn will disappear, or grow down in the quarter, in which case the farrier should fit a bor shoe, so as to throw the weight off the diseased heel and partly on the frog, the elastic surface of which will prevent severe pressure.

If a horse has a long foot, the pressure is more on the corns, because his foot is in front of him, and an over-proportion of his weight comes on his heels. A horse with a long foot is like a man with a thick

No. 15.

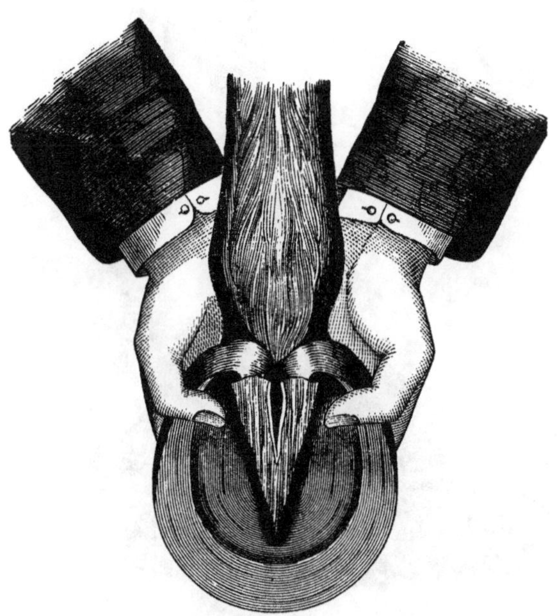

EXPANDING THE FOOT AFTER IT HAS BEEN PARED OUT.

No. 16.

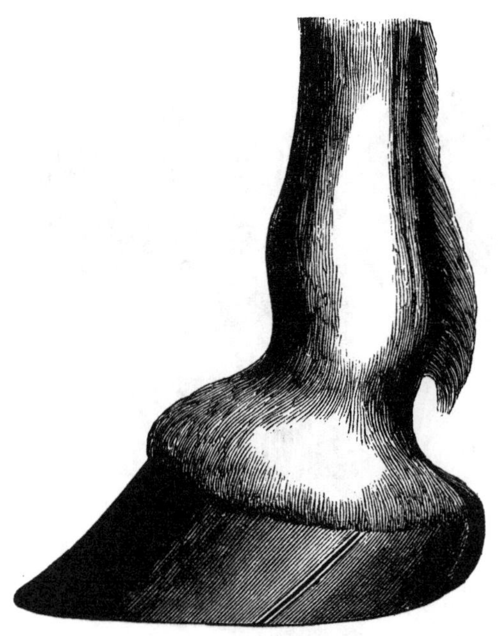

LATERAL QUARTER CRACK BEFORE TREATMENT. CONTRACTED FOOT.

No. 17.

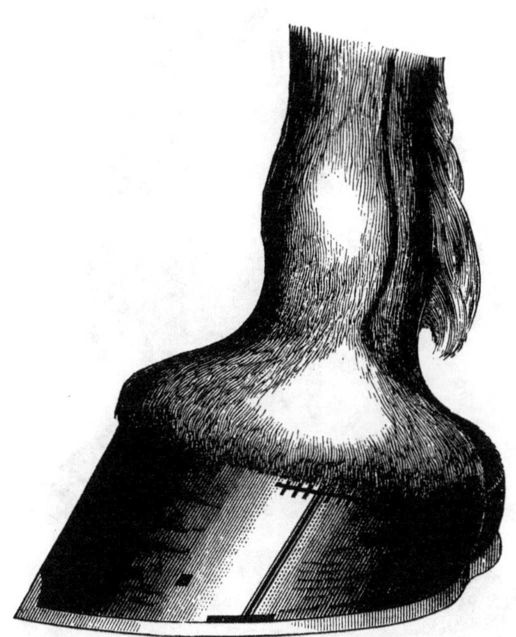

Quarter Crack—Lateral—Under Treatment.

No. 18.

STRAIGHT QUARTER CRACK UNDER TREATMENT.

sole to his boot and no heels, for he strikes the ground first.

Every horse should have his feet well *under* him, and not in *front* of him. This fact should be taken into consideration when fitting the open shoe.

Inflammation should be reduced by placing a swab over the cornet, and using a hot poultice of linseed meal for the foot.

The pressure having been removed from a corn for a fortnight, it will be observed to have a light color, representing the color of a new corn, and if properly treated, it will gradually disappear, and be displaced by a healthy growth of foot.

The horse should be allowed at least a month in which to recover from his lameness; but it is not necessary to turn him out to grass, and care should be taken that his feet are closely attended to, having the shoes renewed about once in a fortnight.

Contraction is the result of neglect, want of natural moisture, and tight shoeing. The result is lameness, if in one foot, and if in both feet, the loss of their free, natural use, causing short steps and stumbling

If the inner quarter is contracted, it is the cause, if not soon remedied, of quarter-crack. The practice of fitting a shoe so as to fit tighter on the inner than the outer quarter, to prevent interfering, renders it more liable to contraction.

The want of proper moisture causes the horn to shrink, and prevents the foot from expanding naturally. This should be remedied by soaking the feet, if feverish, in warm, and if healthy, in cold water, twice a day, an hour at each time. This moisture should be applied at least two hours before the horse is used. This will render the foot elastic, and prevent abuse from travelling over rough roads.

By reference to accompanying plate, No. 12, the difference will be observed between a natural and a contracted foot. The quarters growing toward each other in the contracted, cause the coffin-bone to lose its proper shape, and forcing the sensitive frog upwards from its proper place, causes scratches and thrush.

Treatment of contraction, briefly speaking, is *expansion*. The foot should be

No. 19.

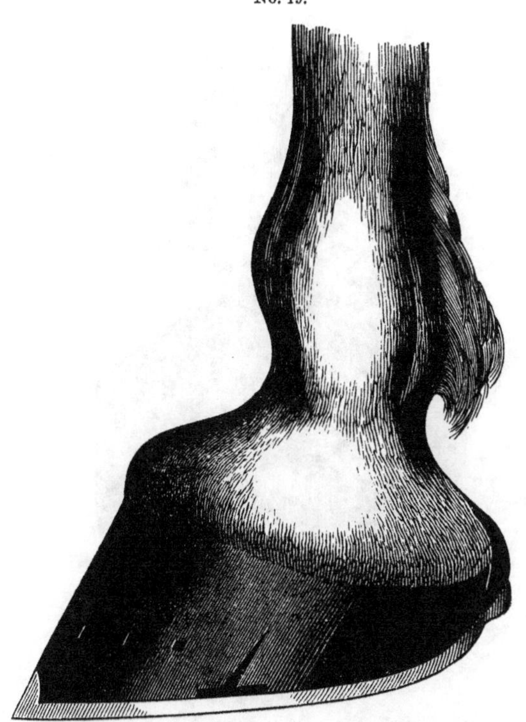

QUARTER CRACK, AFTER TREATMENT.

No. 20.

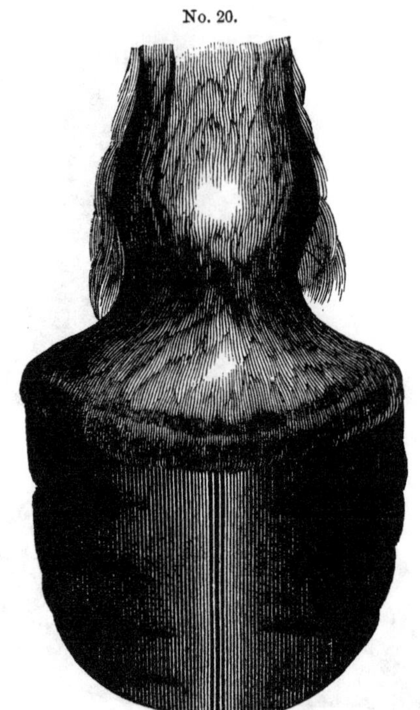

TOE CRACK, BEFORE TREATMENT.

thoroughly prepared in the following manner: If the horse is lame, the farrier should shorten the toe, lower the foot all around, and open the heels back until the blood is drawn. The sole of the foot should be pared as closely as possible on each side of the frog, in the manner shown by the illustration on Plate No. 12, "natural foot." The frog should be lowered, but the side should *not* be cut. A groove should be made with a rasp just under and parallel with the cornet on each side (see Plate No. 14) deep enough to draw blood, then with a fine shoeing knife, cut little notches down from the cornet and across the groove at certain equal distances, as shown by illustration No. 14, the entire length of the groove. These notches should also be deep enough to draw blood. This will relieve the pressure caused by contraction from the cartilages on both sides, and allow them to resume their proper shape.

Having the foot ready for a shoe, a hand should be placed on each side of the foot, pressing it outward in the manner shown by Plate No. 15. The shoe must be very carefully fitted, and must have eight nail-holes, for the reason that it is the heel nails that relieve a horse while in contraction.

The shoe should be fitted so as to project at least a quarter of an inch on each side of the foot, so as to see the nail-holes projecting on each side of the outer and inner quarter. Having this accomplished, the bearing should be equal; the nails must be driven first toward the toe, then toward the heel, driving them half way, and using the utmost care and skill; the higher the nails are driven the better. The shoe being fitted so wide, there is no fear of pricking.

The nails toward the heel should be driven by alternate taps on each side, because the foot expands on each side on account of being pared so thin on either side of the frog, the source of the expansion.

The heel nails should relieve the wings of the coffin-bone, which suffer most while in a state of contraction, and allow them to come back to their proper position.

Considerable soreness will result from this mode of treatment, which can be remedied by using thin poultices of linseed meal, applied as hot as possible, to be renewed at least once every two days for the period of two weeks. The foot should also be thoroughly soaked in a bucket of warm water for half an hour at each renewal of the poultice; this will remove all soreness, and prevent the foot from shrinking when exposed to the weather. The *expansion* treatment should be continued gradually until the coffin-bone resumes its natural shape; when this is accomplished, the growing hoof will naturally accommodate itself to the bone.

The severe treatment recommended is necessary only in an aggravated case causing lameness. It can be so modified by cutting the hoof, and expanding the foot gradually, as to allow the horse to be used while under treatment, if he has not been disabled.

QUARTER AND TOE-CRACKS.

Quarter-cracks are commonly found in feet of saddle horses, and are caused by contraction and pressure, and are also the result of a shoe being fitted tightly on the inner quarter, to prevent interfering, as stated in remarks on "Contraction."

Most commonly found on the inner quarter; it commences at the cornet, extending downward, and when it extends through to the laminæ causes lameness, and is especially serious if the foot is contracted, as shown by Plate No. 16.

There are two kinds of quarter-cracks, as shown by Plates Nos. 17 and 18—the *lateral* and the straight, the latter being the most serious, if the separation commences at the cornet.

Treatment.—If the foot is inclined to contract, it should be prepared as for contraction; shorten the toe and expand the foot, under the directions already given. If lameness has resulted, a bor shoe should be fitted, so as to remove all pressure from half an inch on each side of the crack. Then with a rasp cut a groove under and parallel with the cornet, extending about half an inch on each side of the crack; with a shoeing knife cut some small notches

No. 21.

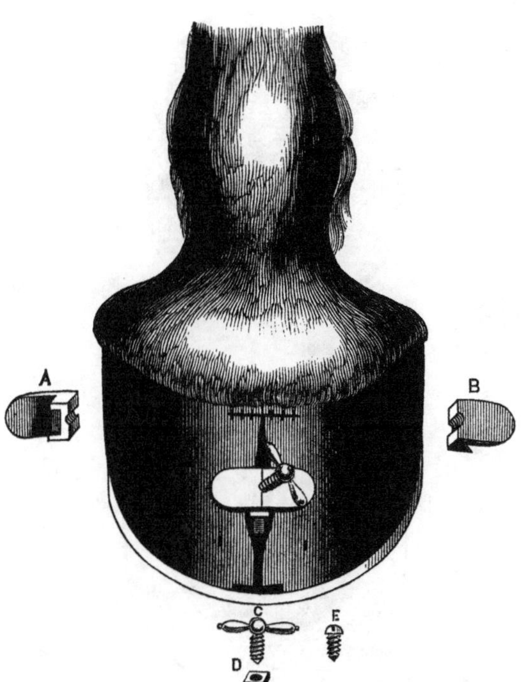

Toe Crack, after Treatment.

Explaining use of "Expansion Plate."

No. 22.

THRUSH—BEFORE TREATMENT.

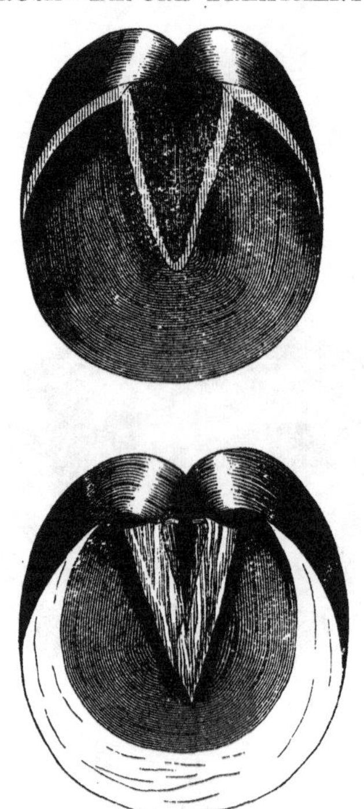

AFTER TREATMENT.

No. 23.

BEFORE TREATMENT—PUMICE FOOT.

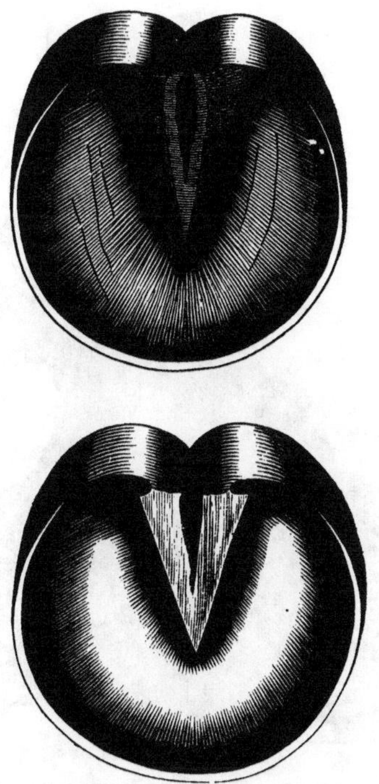

AFTER TREATMENT.

No. 24.

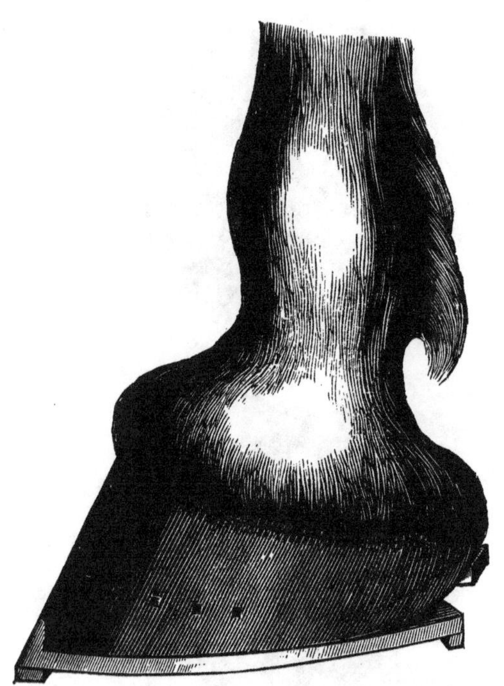

HOOFBOUND—UNDER TREATMENT.

on each side of the groove, after which the edges of the crack may be cut away. (See Plates Nos. 17 and 18.) If the foot bleeds freely so much the better. After this is done a firing-iron should be applied so as to cauterize the crack. This operation having been performed, the foot should be dressed with tar every morning for about three weeks. The pressure being removed, the new growth will commence at the cornet, and extend downward, as shown in Plate No. 19, until a permanent cure is effected.

Toe-crack, more common to heavy and draught horses, is caused by want of room; the space inside the wall of the foot not being large enough to accommodate the laminæ, it causes inflammation, and breaks out at the weakest point, which is the cornet, and extends downward to the toe, causing the foot to assume the appearance of a cloven foot. (See Plate No. 20.)

Treatment.—Shorten the toe as much as possible, and then pare the sole of the foot until it will yield to the pressure of the thumb. No pressure should be allowed within half an inch on each side of the crack on the toe, for the reason that the pressure on the toe prevents the cornet from uniting. Having prepared the sole of the foot, a fine shoeing knife should be used to remove the horn that is inclined to grow inward on each side of the crack, after which a groove under the cornet, extending on each side of the crack, will be made, and the notches on each side of the groove, as already directed. A firing-iron should be applied to cauterize the crack from the cornet downward. Then the crack should be cut away in the centre, so as to allow the use of an "expansion plate," as shown in Plate No. 21. This expansion plate can be made of brass or steel. It is composed of four pieces, as follows: A plate divided in the centre into two equal parts, A and B (see Plate No. 21), and a thread cut in the centre. Each part is made so as to fit dove-tailed into the crack, held in place with a screw C, and a burr D, underneath, to prevent the screw from pressing the laminæ of the foot. The screw, which has considerable power as a lever, forces the two plates apart, lifts up the wall of the foot which is pressing each side of the crack, and presses it outward. This being done, an open shoe should be fitted, wider than the foot, so as to expand it, which, together with the notches cut in the groove under the cornet, will cause a new and strong growth from each side of the crack, commencing at the cornet and extending downward.

The length of time required to effect a removal of the crack depends on the treatment and skill of the operator. If the foot is expanded by the plate with skill, and the nails in the shoe driven so as to prevent the wall of the foot from closing in on the crack, the plate may be removed at once; otherwise it should remain stationary, which can be done by substituting the small screw E, which will not prevent the horse from being used while under treatment. The use of the expansion plate is not necessary, unless the crack extends the whole length of the hoof. The crack extending from the cornet, partly down the front of the foot, should be treated at once, removing pressure by shortening the toe and expanding the foot, as already instructed; then, by means of the groove and notches, promote a new growth at the cornet.

THRUSH

Is a disease of the frog, most common to a foot which is hoof-bound or contracted, but all horses' feet are subject to it when they are neglected. The frog, pressed on each side by the bors of the foot, and from the overgrowth of the hoof, becomes inflamed, and the result is *thrush.* (See Plate No. 22.)

Treatment if the Hoof is Hoof-bound.—The farrier, after removing the shoe, should use his rasp, and lower the wall of the foot all around from heel to heel; then, by the free use of the knife, pare the foot to its natural size. Also pare around the frog until the sole of the foot yields to the pressure of the thumb, then open the heels and remove the pegs that grow on each side of the heels. All this should be done before a knife is used on the frog. After

No. 25.

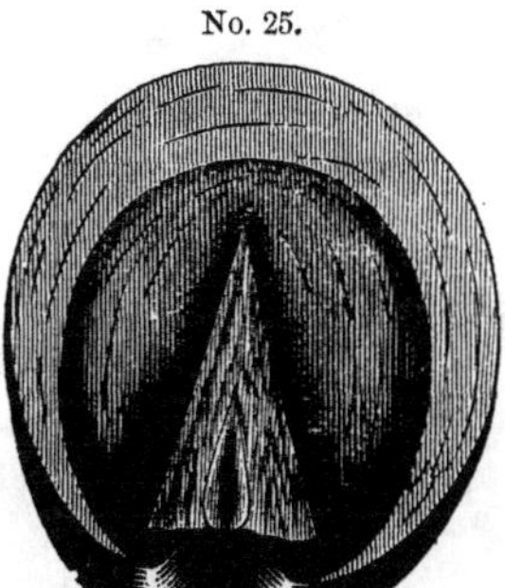

AFTER TREATMENT.

No. 25.

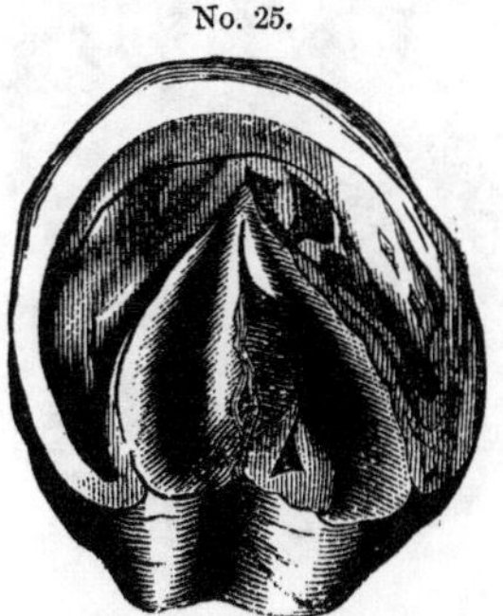

OVERGROWTH OF HOOF AND NEGLECT.

Ground Surface before Treatment.

No. 26.

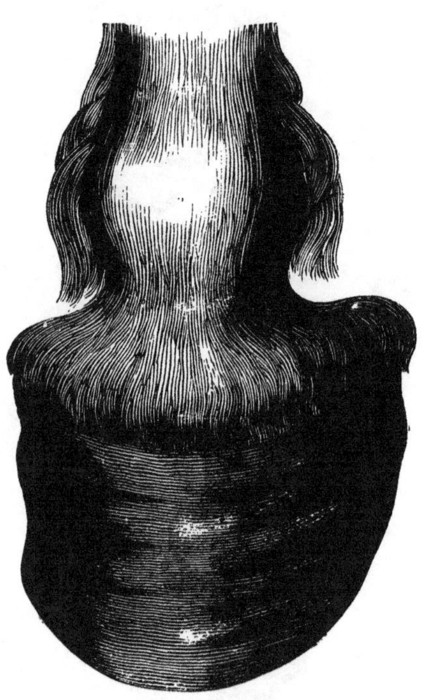

OVERGROWTH OF HOOF—FRONT VIEW BEFORE TREATMENT.

No. 27.

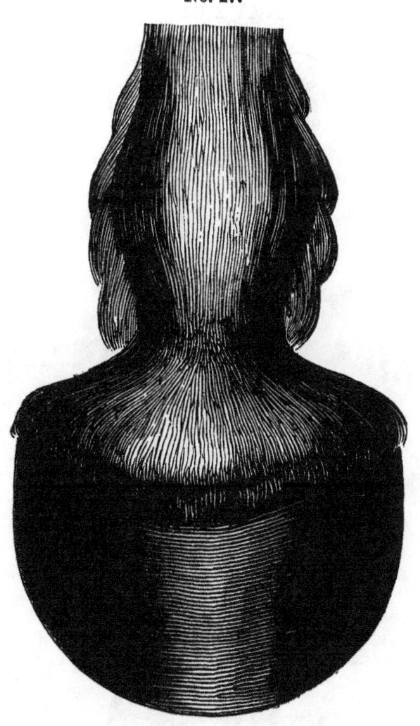

Overgrowth of Hoof—Front View after Treatment.

No. 28.

NAVICULA.

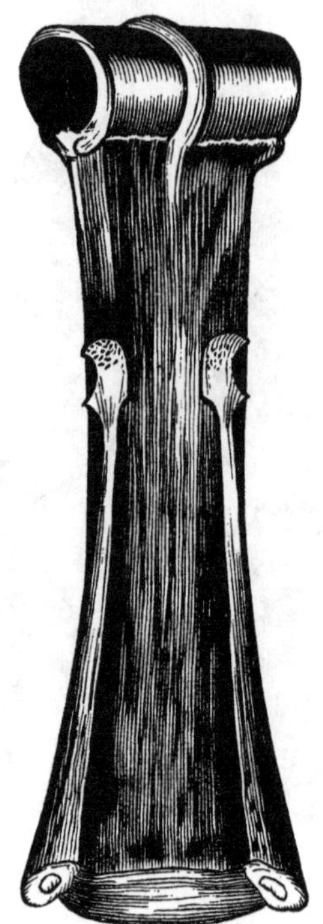

ENLARGEMENT OF METACARPAL BONE.

all pressure is removed by this paring operation, the condition of the frog will show how it was affected by pressure on each side.

Next, by the use of the knife, cut a slice off the top of the frog, and carefully clean out the cleft, which suffers most on account of the direct pressure of the bors on each side of the frog. After this cleaning operation is performed, a warm poultice of flaxseed meal should be applied two or three times, according to the condition of the foot. When the poultice is removed, the foot should be washed out occasionally with castile soap and warm water, after which a little salt, ground into fine powder, should be forced into the cleft, and kept in by a mixture of tar and oakum as a dressing, after which an open shoe should be fitted so as to expand the foot gradually. This treatment should be pursued until a permanent cure is effected.

If the foot is in a state of contraction, it should be expanded under the instructions already given. By this expansion all pressure is removed, and a permanent cure is easily effected by following the instructions already given.

No liquid remedies, such as butter of antimony, or chloride of zinc, should be used, as they dry up the foot before the inflammation is removed.

By reference to Plate No. 22 a good idea may be obtained of the manner of paring out a hoof suffering from thrush.

PUMICE FOOT

(See Plate No. 23), should always be pared out on each side of the frog until it yields to the pressure of the thumb. This paring should, however, be done immediately around the frog, leaving more than the usual ground surface (see plate After Treatment). The toe should be shortened as much as possible, and the heels cut out back. If the horse is lame a bor shoe is the best to protect the foot, with a leather sole, and some tar as a moisture. This shoe should be renewed at least once a month, with a leather sole, until a cure is effected.

HOOF-BOUND.

(Plate No. 24.) A horse that is hoof-bound is deprived of his free action, and resembles a horse that is foundered.

Treatment.—The foot should be pared out thoroughly, and on each side of the frog, until it yields to the pressure of the thumb. Open the heels and remove the bors that press the frog on each side, and cause the animal much pain.

The toe should be shortened, and if the foot is inclined to contraction, the shoe should be fitted wider than the foot, which if done properly will expand the foot (see article Contraction). The shoe should be a good, heavy, open one, well eased off at the heels. Having the foot prepared, the operation should next be performed around the cornet, as follows: If the cartilages are hard, as they are generally from being pressed upwards, a groove should be made with a rasp immediately under the cornet, and extending all the way across from heel to heel, deep enough to draw blood. Next, with a fine knife cut notches across the groove at equal distances the whole length of the groove, and extending from the cornet downward.

By this operation, illustrated on Plate No. 24, the pressure is removed from the cartilages. After this a poultice of linseed meal should be applied around the cornet, which loosens all pressure and starts a new growth.

If the horse is lame from this disease the close cutting operation should be performed and the poultice applied one week; otherwise the operation need not be so severe.

PLATES Nos. 25, 26, 27—*Illustrations of Overgrowth of Hoof and Neglect before and after Treatment.*—The illustration, "Before Treatment," Plate No. 25, represents the ground surface of a foot operated upon, and "After Treatment" represents the same foot after one pound of overgrowth had been removed from one foot. Plates Nos. 26 and 27 show the difference between the foot before and after treatment, and show the importance of being careful in observing a horse's foot so as to prevent lameness, and the various diseases caused by neglect.

PLATES NOS. 28 AND 29—*Enlargement of the Metacarpal Bone.*—In a great many cases because the enlargement interferes with the free use of the flexor tendon pressing it out of its proper place. A horse with a contracted foot suffers from this pressure when the shoe is fitted tight and brings the heels inward. The metacarpal bones extend from the back of the knee downward to the pastern joint, forming, as it were, a brace on each side. They become quite small as they extend downward, and the enlargement is generally found on the inside of the leg (see Plate No. 28).

The enlargement may be discovered by running the hand downward from the knee, the thumb on one side and the fore finger on the other, until it is felt (see Plate 29, "A"). If pressed and the horse yields to the pressure, it is a sure sign that he is affected, and he should be properly shod at once as if for contraction, or the enlargement should be removed. To do this, the horse should be in the following position:

No. 29.

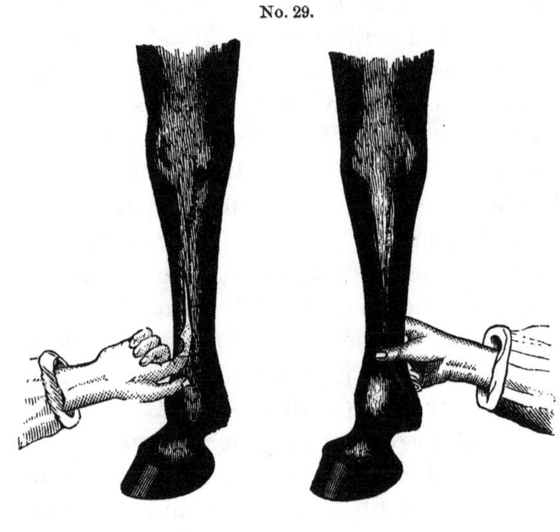

b *a*

ENLARGEMENT OF THE METACARPAL BONE.

a Showing how to find the enlargement.

b Showing the manner in which the incision is made, and the enlargement removed.

First, with plenty of straw under him, to prevent bruising; then he should be thrown on his side and fastened down, so as to allow the operator to make an incision with a fine pocket knife partly to the front and near where the enlargement is. This operation will not interfere with the tendons, or veins that extend upward from the foot. The incision having been made, the finger may be inserted, as shown in Plate No. 29, "B," so as to raise the enlargement and make it visible. Then, with a pair of nippers, snap the end off with one motion. The incision should be closed, fastened together with a needle and silk thread; then apply a linen bandage and over this a woollen cloth, containing a little moisture, to prevent fever. A little sweet oil should be applied, to keep it clean while healing. The operation is not severe and is thoroughly effective.

PLATES NOS. 30 AND 31 represent a foot which has been deprived of the free use of the back tendons, caused by a sudden jar or misstep, causing a horse so affected to travel on his toe, and can be remedied

No. 30.

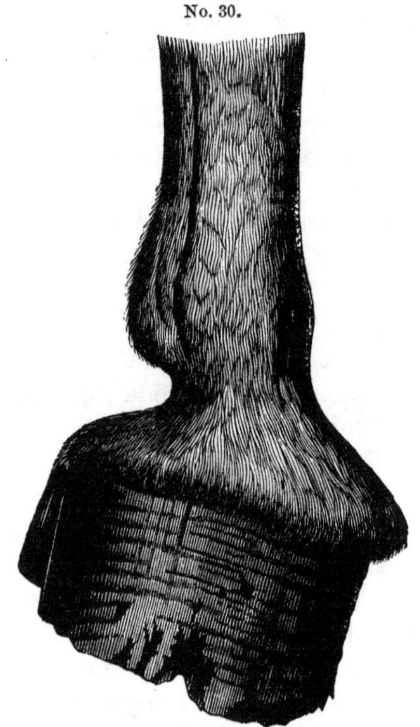

A Foot that is Deprived of the free use of the Back Tendons.

No. 31.

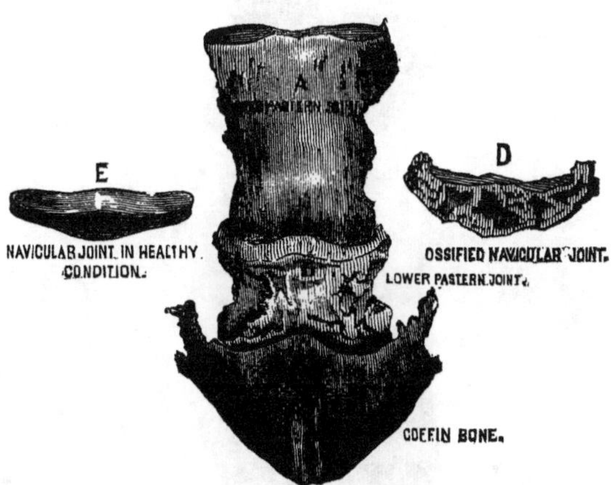

Ossified growth of Upper and Lower Pastern Joint, also Navicular Joint and Coffin-bone, in a foot which has been deprived of the free use of the back Tendons. See Plate No. 30.

No. 32.

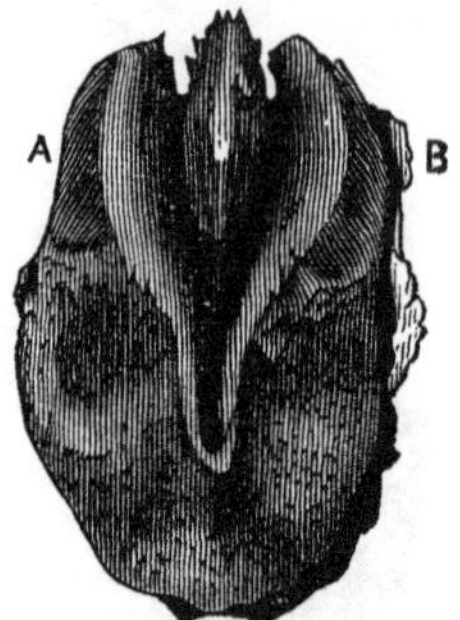

Interior surface.

No. 32.

Exterior surface.

THE SENSITIVE FROG.

No. 33.

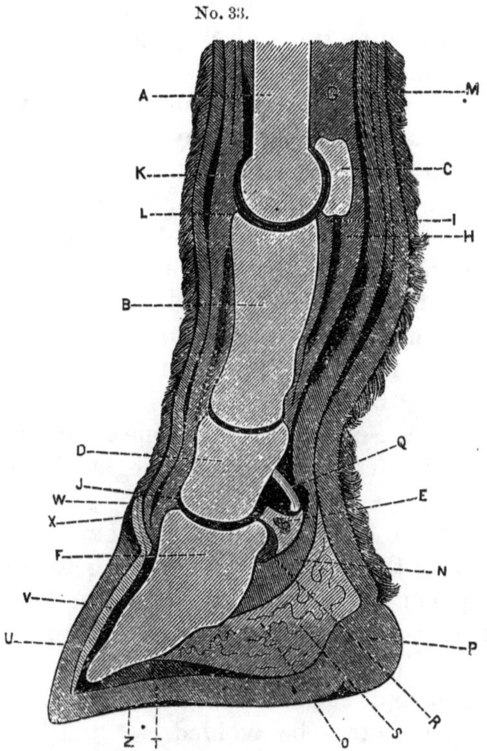

SECTION OF THE PASTERN AND OTHER BONES, LIGAMENTS, ETC.

only by a system of expanding the foot under the directions already given for contraction.

After this a shoe should be fitted with a toe and no heels, for by raising the toe the bearing is thrown on the heels. If the action is heavy on the toe, the shoe should be provided with a steel toe calk. This will prevent a horse from travelling on his toe, and such a case, if taken in time, can be remedied, if not permanently cured, by simply fitting a shoe so as to throw the bearing on the heels.

Plates Nos. 30 and 31 represent an aggravated case, which from neglect became incurable.

Plate No. 32 represents the exterior surface of the sensitive frog. The great principle of this system of paring the horse's feet, is to remove all pressure from the frog. It should be protected from all pressure, and such diseases as thrush and scratches may be avoided.

Plate No. 33 gives a sectional view of all the bones and tendons of the horse's foot. Every blacksmith and farrier should thoroughly understand this and the anatomy of the horse's foot, in order to be able to know exactly how to treat any disease which may be brought to their notice.

A—Shank-bone.
B—Upper and larger pastern-bone.
C—Sesamoid-bone.
D—Lower or smaller pastern-bone.
E—Navicular or shuttle-bone.
F—Coffin-bone, or bone of the foot.
G—Suspensory ligament inserted into the sesamoid-bone.
H—Continuation of the suspensory ligament inserted into the smaller pastern-bone.
I—Small inelastic ligament lying down the sesamoid-bone to the larger pastern-bone.
K—A long ligament reaching from the pastern-bone to the knee.
L—Extensor tendon inserted into both the pastern and the coffin-bone.
M—Tendon of the perforating flexor inserted into the coffin-bone, after having passed over the navicular-bone.
N—Seat of the navicular joint lameness.
O—Inner or sensible frog.
P—Cleft of the horny frog.
Q—A ligament uniting the navicular-bone to the smaller pastern.
R—A ligament uniting the navicular-bone to the coffin-bone.
S—Sensible sole between the coffin-bone and the horny side.
T—Horny sole.
U—Crust or wall of the foot.
V—Sensible laminæ to which the crust is attached.
W—Coronary ring of the crust.
X—The covering of the coronary ligament from which the crust is secreted.
Z—Place of bleeding at the toe.

www.ingramcontent.com/pod-product-compliance
Lightning Source LLC
LaVergne TN
LVHW011205110826
845150LV00006B/1323

* 9 7 8 1 4 2 5 5 1 8 5 7 8 *